Sensory Play

Over 65 Sensory Bin Topics with Picture Books, Supplementary Activities, and Snacks for a Complete Toddler Program

Gayle Jervis & Kristen Jervis Cacka

Copyright © 2013 Kristen Jervis Cacka

All rights reserved.

ISBN-10: 1492876445
ISBN-13: 978-1492876441

No part of this publication may be used or reproduced in any form or by any means, electronic or mechanical, including photocopying, recording, or by an information storage and retrieval systems without written permission of the publisher or author (except by a reviewer, who may quote brief passages in a review).

DEDICATION

To our Husbands who have supported our ideas!

CONTENTS

	Introduction	1
1.	Sensory Bin Essentials	11
2.	Color Sensory Bins	29
3.	Season Sensory Bins	75
4.	Celebration Sensory Bins	115
5.	Alphabetical or Topical Sensory Bins	163
	Other Books	247
	About The Authors	248
	Works Cited	250
	Index	260

DISCLAIMER

The authors and the publisher cannot be held responsible for damage, mishap, injury incurred during the use of or because of activities in this book. Appropriate and reasonable caution and adult supervision of children involved in activities and corresponding to the age and capability of each child involved is recommended at all times. Do not leave children unattended at any time. Observe safety and caution at all times. While all attempts have been made to provide effective, verifiable information in this book, neither the author nor publisher assumes responsibility for errors, inaccuracies or omissions.

INTRODUCTION

Each day I live in a glass room unless I break it with the thrusting of senses and pass through the splintered walls to the great landscape.

- Mervyn Peake

If you have a toddler, you already know that your child needs many opportunities to explore his surroundings or he will get into trouble finding his own things to touch, smell, taste, observe and feel! Sensory bins provide those controlled opportunities to help your child better interact with and understand his world. You may already be giving your child finger paints, play dough and other sensory experiences and wonder whether you need to add sensory bins to his activities. Those activities are all important, and were included in our first book Busy Toddler, Happy Mom. However, we also gave our readers some examples of sensory bins, and because they provide so many benefits to your child's development, we decided to write a book on how to use sensory bins on a regular basis.

BENEFITS OF USING SENSORY BINS:

First, you are giving your child opportunities to assume the role of scientist as she handles, manipulates, sorts and explores all the items that are in the sensory bin.

Second, you are increasing your child's attentiveness. These bins will hold your child's interest longer than many other toddler activities. Your child will be fascinated with the potpourri of items that you have added to his bin and he will enjoy making decisions on how he wants to use them.

Third, you are developing your child's small motor skills as she learns how to use tongs, tweezers, eye droppers, and funnels.

Fourth, you are giving her opportunities to develop her creativity every time she decides what to do with each item in the bin.

Fifth, after his own self discoveries, these bins give you opportunities to introduce new concepts to your child such as how to use tongs, or introduce new vocabulary, or show him how to sort.

Sixth, you are giving your child opportunities to develop her five senses that child researchers believe are essential to develop at a young age. However, fiction writers and poets also have something to say about the importance of our senses:

Touch comes before sight, before speech. It is the first language and the last, and it always tells the truth.

- Margaret Atwood

For ourselves, who are ordinary men and women, let us return thanks to Nature for her bounty by using every one of the senses she has given us.

- Virginia Woolf

Senses empower limitations, senses expand vision within borders, senses promote understanding through pleasure.

- Dejan Stojanovic

Seventh, sensory bins provide a great medium for interacting with your child and for enjoying each other's company.

Eighth, sensory bins create opportunities for younger and older children to cooperate and work together. Therefore, they are great activities for siblings!

Ninth, all these benefits occur while your child is playing and having fun!

TYPES OF SENSORY BINS

The sensory bins are divided into four categories:
1. Color Sensory Bins
2. Season Sensory Bins
3. Celebration Sensory Bins
4. Alphabetical or Topical Sensory Bins

The easiest bin to put together is the <u>Color Sensory Bins</u> and that may be the first one you will want to try. However, remember that many colors are being introduced and that these bins are only introductions to a topic that will be gradually learned.

For the <u>Season Sensory Bins</u>, three sensory bins per season have been included. Each bin focuses on one particular aspect of that season. You may decide to introduce a season by using all three bins in one month or you may gradually introduce a particular season during the next three months.

The <u>Celebration Sensory Bins</u> has a celebration for each month of the year. Again, remember that your child's understanding of these celebrations is limited so that these bins are merely an introduction to what your child will better understand when he becomes a preschooler.

Finally, the <u>Alphabetical or Topical Sensory Bins</u> are not limited to introducing your child to letters of the alphabet. In fact, your child will likely not be ready to distinguish any letters especially if he is younger than 2 1/2 years old. These bins can be used when your child is older and ready to learn his uppercase and lower case letters. In the meantime, introduce the topic that is being used for each letter. He can still enjoy a bin about ants and not understand that ants begin with the letter "a".

ACTIVITIES TO SUPPLEMENT SENSORY BINS:

A variety of activities have been included to increase your child's understanding of the topic and help deepen his experience with the sensory bin. However, these sensory bins can be used independently and your child will still receive all those benefits that have been listed.

FURTHER ENRICHMENT: Before you begin each sensory category, you will find a list of suggestions to enrich your child's enjoyment of this topic. For example, there will be ideas how to use play dough after your child's explorations with her sensory bin.

PICTURE BOOKS: These books were chosen to increase your child's enjoyment of his sensory bin. For example, before he explores the bin for skating, he will read some books about skating such as Skating Day by Mercer Mayer. As you point out various pictures and read the story, you will be giving him new vocabulary for that theme. This better understanding of the topic will increase his creativity when he begins to play with the items in the bin.

Please note that you don't need to read all the books listed. Just choose one or two books from the list that you can find in your local library.

SUPPLEMENTARY ACTIVITY: These activities will build on her discoveries from the bin. For example, after your child has enjoyed her Garden Sensory Bin, you will help her plant grass seeds in a plastic cup.

SNACK: Your toddler's sense of taste will generally not be used when he plays with the sensory bin. Therefore, we have incorporated simple snack ideas that reflect the specific theme. For example, in one of the summer bins, you will be looking at fish. You could make some blue Jello and when it is slightly thickened, add some Gold Fish Crackers.

Toddlers require a variety of activities to keep their active minds stimulated. We believe you will be very happy to see how well sensory bins occupy your toddler's attention and how all these extra activities will maintain her attentiveness and will continue to stimulate her curiosity.

May you and your toddler have great times together as you begin your sensory journey!

Gayle Jervis & Kristen Jervis Cacka

CHAPTER 1:
SENSORY BIN ESSENTIALS

Gayle Jervis & Kristen Jervis Cacka

A Sensory Bin is a variety of materials placed together to stimulate the senses.

CREATING SENSORY BINS

CHOOSING A CONTAINER:

First, determine how many children will be using the bin. My daughter and I tend to use an under the bed plastic container since we often have two toddlers together playing in it. If your toddler has siblings, assume that they will show an interest in this activity and choose a container large enough to prevent fights. If it is only one child, you can comfortably use a smaller but shallow rectangular container. The advantage of using the under the bed container is that it usually has wheels and can be easily stored under a bed.

Second, change your container occasionally to pique your child's interest. Use any sand or water tables that you may have stored away for only summer use. Other options are bowls, cardboard boxes, old suitcases, and various plastic storage containers. Also, large foil roasting pans are great supplements to your child's bins. However, their use is limited as the main container since they don't have lids for storage.

Third, some sensory bins need smaller containers that fit in your larger bin. Choose unbreakable items such as only plastic containers, baskets, bowls or ice cube trays.

CHOOSING A FILLER:

First, most bins have something that your child can shovel, rake or pour. This item is your filler or the base to your sensory bin. It will usually be one of the following:

>   Bird Seed
>   Black Beans
>   Lentils
>   Water Beads
>   Rice
>   Pasta (Different shapes)
>   Split Peas
>   White Coarse Salt
>   Shredded Paper
>   Play Sand

These items can usually be bought in bulk to keep your cost down.

Water Beads can usually be found at a craft store in the floral section or purchased online at http://waterbeadscanada.net.

Second, we give you many ideas to use as fillers but use whatever fillers you have available or whatever you find is cheapest. If we suggest shredding red construction paper and you want to use red colored rice, do so. To cut back on costs, you may decide to buy only white rice and merely add the specific colored items for your bin.

Third, add any essential oil or cooking extracts to the filler to increase your child's sensory experience. For example, use vanilla extract, peppermint extract, almond extract, baby oil, lavender oil, etc.

Fourth, each filler can be reused in various bins offsetting the filler's initial cost. For example, bird feed is recommended for the Farm bin and for the Thanksgiving bin.

Fifth, for added visual appeal, use colored rice or pasta. The recipe for colored rice or colored pasta is as follows:

> *Recipe for Colored Rice or Colored Pasta*
> 12 cups of White Rice
> 8 Tbsp Rubbing Alcohol
> Bottle of Food Coloring

If you have a large roasting pan, you could add all the rice at one time. Otherwise, just make the rice in portions. Add 4 cups of the rice, 2 Tbsp of rubbing alcohol and 1/3 of the bottle of food coloring in one large bowl and mix together. Spread on a cookie sheet. Do this three more times to make your 12 cups of rice. Then leave on the counter overnight to make sure it is fully dry. Don't be concerned about the smell of the rubbing alcohol since after the rice is dry, the smell disappears.

CHOOSING MANIPULATIVES:

Provide a variety of items beside the sensory bin that your child will use to explore its contents. These items will be used most often to play with the filler. For each sensory bin, try to provide something different to stimulate his curiosity and develop his small motor skills. Here is a list of suggestions:

> Tongs
> Sieves
> Spoons of Various Sizes
> Ladles

Aquarium Net
Watering Can
Whisk
Baster
Eyedroppers
Large Tweezers
Muffin Tins
Egg Cartons
Shovels
Pails
Funnels of Various Sizes
Small Child's Rake

CHOOSING TOPICAL ITEMS:

For each sensory bin, you will need a variety of topical items. The easiest topic will be the Color Sensory Bins since most of those items you probably have in your home. When you are studying a topic that your child already enjoys such as dinosaurs, again you will just use your child's toys. However, there will be other bins that will require some items to be purchased. For example, when you do the Valentine's Day Bin, you will most likely need to go to a Dollar Store or a Craft Store and pick up appropriate items. However, take note of what bins you will be doing in the next few months so that you can buy them ahead of time when they are on sale. Also, remember that many of these items can be used again for other bins.

STORING ITEMS FOR SENSORY BINS

First, store your fillers in large plastic containers or sealable bags for future use.

Second, store the various items that you have bought for these bins so that they will be accessible for later use. Mason jars or sealable bags work well for storing the smaller items you will be collecting. Have jars for such items as fish and other sea creatures, snakes and lizards, dinosaurs, pompoms, Valentine's Day/red items, St. Patrick's Day/green items, and so on.

Third, store your manipulatives, such as various scoops, in a large plastic container.

Even though you have additional household items you could take from your kitchen drawers, it is convenient to have everything readily accessible in this one container.

SENSORY BIN SAFETY

Your child's safety is always the first priority in whatever activity you give to your child. Only you will know whether some of the suggestions are not yet appropriate for your toddler. This will be especially true if you have a toddler younger than two years old as he may still be putting things into his mouth. **<u>Do not leave the room at anytime while your toddler is playing with his sensory bin</u>**. Even a quick departure gives him time to either make an incredible mess with the bird feed or decide to feed the bird feed to your pet or decide at that moment to check out its taste.

HOW TO HANDLE MESS

As parents, we sometimes focus more on cleanness than on our child's development. However, it is possible to maintain a tidy home and work on your child's sensory development if you follow some simple ways to handle any mess:

1. Place a plastic table cloth on the floor under the sensory bin and around the play area.
2. Teach your toddler to keep all the items contained within the drop cloth on the floor.
3. Teach your toddler to help you when an accident or an exuberant play moment causes too much of the filler and items to land on the floor.
4. When your child is finished playing, put the lid on it, and don't allow your child to play with it unless he has your permission.
5. Convey to your child that it is a privilege to play with the sensory bin

and when she doesn't follow the rules, just quietly remove the bin.

HOW TO INTRODUCE SENSORY BINS

First, decide what bins you will want to do for a month. If you would like to give your toddler a new sensory bin each week, then you may want to choose one from each category for the month: Seasons, Colors, Celebrations, and Alphabet/Topical. If you have an older toddler, you may decide to focus more on the Alphabet Sensory Bins and occasionally add one from the other categories. There is no right way - choose bins that you think will capture your toddler's interest. Also, choose bins that may overlap so that you won't need to buy as many items. For example, a Red Color Bin could be used in February when you also planning to do the Valentine's Day Bin. Similarly, do the Green Color Sensory Bin the same month you are doing the St. Patrick's Day Bin.

Second, choose clothing for your toddler to stimulate his interest in the bin you have assembled. If you are giving him a Colors Bin, then help him find clothes in that color. If he is exploring dinosaurs, does he have a shirt or a pair of pyjamas that has a picture of dinosaurs on it? Does he have a pirate's costume he could wear when he is exploring the Pirate's Treasure Bin?

Third, change the way you give the bin to your toddler. Sometimes, include all the items at one time for a fun visual experience. Other times, give him a container that has only the filler so that he can focus on pouring this filler into other containers or pouring it into various funnels. Then when he begins to lose interest, add some of the thematic items. This method can often prolong his involvement with the bin.

Fourth, stay out of the way so that he can make his own discoveries!

Fifth, you will need to do some experimenting

and observing as you tweak each bin for your child's ultimate enjoyment. For example, I thought my "Grand Toddlers" would love to play with the straw I had bought for their farm bin, but they tended to avoid it. Later, when they played with this bin, they were drawn to the straw only after I took a bunch of it out. Apparently, there was too much in it and the animals didn't want to stand on top of the hay!

LEARNING MOMENTS

There are many learning opportunities that arise through these bins, but much of that learning actually occurs without your interaction.

However, when there are indications that your toddler is tiring of his own explorations, it may be a good time to have a few learning moments with your child. Here are some suggestions:

1. Develop his vocabulary by naming certain items that are in the bin. Ask him to find the named item for you. For instance, he may not know the names of all the animals in his Safari Bin and you can begin naming them. He can place the one you have named in a basket.
2. Help her learn to follow directions. For example, you may ask her to take the animal you have named and put it on a hill you have created in the bin.
3. Give him opportunities to sort. For example, when he is playing with his Valentine's Day Bin, give him two small Valentine's Day buckets - one pink and the other red. Have him place all the red hearts in the red bucket and the pink hearts in the pink bucket.
4. Give your older toddler opportunities to count. Have her collect the necklaces that you placed in his Pirate's Treasure Bin and count them.
5. Help him develop his small motor skills. For example, he may not have

used the tongs that you included in the bin since he wasn't sure how to use them. Demonstrate how to use them and show him how to grab hold of such items as pompoms

6. Add to your toddler's enjoyment and understanding of one of the picture books you have read to her as she plays in her bin. For example, when she is exploring her Red Bin and she picks up a red doll boot, you could remind her of the story you read to her called Holly's Red Boots.

7. Help your child develop his observation skills. For example, help him notice that the red rice slips through the wide funnel faster than through the narrow funnel. Have him notice the size of objects, that some are large and others are small. Can he find another item that is large? Help him decide whether an object will fit into a container that you have placed in the bin.

8. Have your toddler make predictions. When she is pouring bird seed into a bucket, ask her if she adds one more shovel full, will the birdseed overflow?

CHAPTER 2:
COLOR SENSORY BINS

Color Sensory Bins are an enjoyable and easy way to begin introducing sensory bins to your child. Before you choose a bin, make sure you read the following suggestions.

BEFORE YOU START THESE BINS:

1. Decide how often you want to introduce these colors to your toddler. You may decide to give your toddler a color sensory bin once a week or once a month.

2. Check out the list of specific books for each color and reserve these ahead of time at your library.
3. If you are reading the suggested color picture books, try to include one or two items mentioned in these books so that you can refer to the story when your child is playing with his sensory bin.

FURTHER ENRICHMENT:

- Start a Colors Photo Album for your toddler. You will need a 4 X 6 photo album. On the first page of the photo book, add a title with your child's name. On one side of the album, insert a 4 X 6 sheet of the construction paper of the appropriate color. On the other side, include the photo of your child wearing something of the same color. It can be as simple as a scarf, toque or socks. Making this book is simple but one that your toddler will enjoy looking at, while at the same time, it provides a great review of the various colors.

- Check out the following website, http://www.kidsparkz.com/colors.html, if you want additional activities to supplement your child's experiences with the sensory bin. For example, your toddler can practice sorting pictures for each color.

As you introduce various colors, make sure you have a selection of colored play dough. For each color that you introduce, you can review by using play dough:

- Hide small items of the color you are studying in a large clump of play dough. Give him tweezers and a small spoon to find them.
- Insert a strand of uncooked spaghetti in a chunk of play dough and give her a small dish of Fruit Loops. Help her find the appropriate color to slip onto the spaghetti.
- Give him some pieces from Mr. and Mrs. Potato Head to add to the specific color of play dough.

- Give her a selection of items in the chosen color to add to her play dough to make a sculpture.
- Make some cupcakes by putting clumps of dough in muffin liners. Give him buttons, beads, candle, sprinkles in the color you are introducing.
- Set out a selection of colorful play dough and flatten them into circles. Then give your toddler a bowl of small items such as buttons and beads to stand up in the play dough.
- Give your toddler cookie cutters in the color that you are introducing to her along with the play dough in that same color.
- If your toddler likes to color, there are various web-sites that provide printable books about specific colors. Check out the following for a circular printable book: <http://www.enchantedlearning.com/themes/colors.shtml> or Single Color Itsy Bitsy Books at <http://www.kidzone.ws/prek_wrksht/colors/single-books.htm>

- You can review each color with this simple activity: Give your toddler a muffin tin and pompoms of the color your are teaching him. Give him tongs to place the pompoms into the muffin tin. Gradually, you can add the number of colors of pompoms and encourage him to sort them into specific tin holders.
- Give your toddler a muffin tin and pompoms of the color you are introducing. Give her tongs to place the pompoms into the muffin tin. Gradually, you can add the number of colors of pompoms and encourage her to sort them into specific tin holders.
- Review any color by giving him that color of pompom and showing him how to blow it on the floor or across a child's table.
- Go on color scavenger hunts after you introduce each color. Use the specific color of pompoms or plastic eggs and hide them in a room.

RED

Red is the great clarifier - bright and revealing. I can't imagine becoming bored with red - it would be like becoming bored with the person you love.

- Diana Vreeland

BOOKS TO READ:
Red, Red, Red by Valeri Gorbachev
Holly's Red Boots by Francesca Chessa
Ten Red Apples by Virginia Miller
Red Hat by Lita Judge
Red Knit Cap Girl by Naoko Stoop
Red Animals by Melissa Stewart
Red: Seeing Red All Around Us by Sarah Schuette

SENSORY BIN:
Color some rice red as your base. (Recipe on Page 16) If you have any Valentine's Day items, use any of the red ones. Also, include any items that you may have that were mentioned in any of the books you read to

your child such as a doll's red boot, and plastic red apples. If you have already bought plastic apples for your Fall Bin, include them. They will be especially good for sorting and for counting. Other red items you can add are plastic strawberries, containers, pompoms, ribbon, buttons, building blocks, and small toys. Remember you can always add some vanilla extract or peppermint extract or an essential oil to the filler to appeal to your child's sense of smell.

SUPPLEMENTARY ACTIVITY:
Make a Red Colors Bottle. You will need an empty plastic bottle or jar. Gatorade bottles work particularly well since they are made of stronger plastic than many other plastic bottles or jars. You will also need a bottle of spray foam shaving cream and red food coloring. Spray the shaving cream into the bottle. Add warm water to fill the bottle with liquid. Shake and watch the foam dissolve. You will probably need to add more water gradually, as you wait for all the foam to

dissolve. Then add your red food coloring. Attach the lid on tightly and give to your toddler. She will love shaking the bottle as the red coloring and the white swirl together.

Check out these videos on YouTube.com:

Children's Color Move - Jazz Baby Red: https://www.youtube.com/watch?v=HCCit_zjNsM

Red Colors for Kids: https://www.youtube.com/watch?v=YX-Du7N7A8A

Meet Mr. Red: http://www.youtube.com/watch?v=nW9P0VE8EmA

SNACK:
Cut a red apple in half taking out its core. If you have an older toddler, give her a plastic knife and show her how to cut slices of apple to put on her plate. You could also give her some red strawberries to eat.

BLUE

Blue is the only color which maintains its own character in all its tones . . . It will always stay blue; whereas yellow is blackened in its shades, and fades away when lightened; red when darkened becomes brown, and diluted with white is no longer red, but another color - pink.

- Raoul Dufy

BOOKS TO READ:
One Sheep Blue Sheep by Thom Wiley
Little Blue Truck by Alice Schertle
Little Blue Truck Leads the Way by Alice Schertle
Blue Animals by Melissa Stewart
Blue Chicken by Deborah Freedman
Blue: Seeing Blue all Around Us by Sarah Schuette
Blue by Philippe Dupasquier

SENSORY BIN:
Make some blue colored pasta. (Recipe on Page 16) If you have any items from some of

the books you have read about blue, make sure you include them. For example, if you have read <u>Little Blue Truck Leads the Way</u>, include a small blue truck. Then begin collecting other blue items: building blocks, pompoms, plastic eggs, colored glass stones, cars, buttons and ribbons.

SUPPLEMENTARY ACTIVITY:
Give your child a blue balloon. Attach a blue ribbon to the balloon and then slip it on to his wrist. If the weather is appropriate, let him enjoy carrying his balloon while going for a walk outside. Otherwise, bounce the balloon back and forth to each other while you sing a corny song about it. For example, sing the following to the tune of Mary Had A Little Lamb:

> We're playing with a blue balloon,
> Blue balloon, blue balloon,
> We're playing with a blue balloon,
> We're having so much fun

Check out this video on YouTube.com:

The Color Blue:
https://www.youtube.com/watch?v=-5IGJS1eT1U

SNACK:

Make some blue Jello and add blueberries. Get your child to help you stir the Jello powder and water. When the Jello has begun to thicken, add the blueberries.

GREEN

Green is the prime color of the world, and that from which its loveliness arises.

- Pedro Calderon de la Barca

BOOKS TO READ:
Little Blue and Little Yellow by Leo Lionni
What Is Green by Kate Endle
A Green, Green Garden by Mercer Mayer
Green Eggs and Ham by Dr. Seuss
My Green Book by Kathy Knowles
Green by Laura Vaccaro Seeger
Green: Seeing Green All Around Us by Sarah Schuette

SENSORY BIN:
Add green split peas to your toddler's sensory bin. For a fragrance, add some lime juice. You may have green items from St. Patrick's Day to add to this bin. Also, add any items that may have been mentioned in any of the books you have read. Include any of the following that are green: pompoms, pipe cleaners,

plastic leaves, toy cars, plastic frogs, buttons, building blocks, and green play food.

SUPPLEMENTARY ACTIVITY:
Tape a paint stirrer to the back of a paper plate. Give your child a green balloon to see if she can carry her balloon on the plate while walking around the room. Then show her how to "bat" the balloon.

Check out this video on Youtube.com:

The Color Green:
https://www.youtube.com/watch?v=OefqQbwb72c

SNACK:
Give your toddler some lightly steamed broccoli and celery to dip into a small dish of Ranch Dressing.

YELLOW

How wonderful yellow is. It stands for the sun.

- Vincent Van Gogh

BOOKS TO READ:
Yellow: Seeing Yellow All Around Us by Sarah Schuette
Yellow Animals by Melissa Stewart
My Yellow Book by Kathy Knowles
Red, Yellow Blue and You by Cynthia Vance
Kitten Red Yellow Blue by Peter Catalanotto
In My New Yellow Shirt by Eileen Spinelli

SENSORY BIN:
Choose large pasta noodles and dye them yellow. (Recipe on Page 16) You could also add some lemon extract to the pasta for your toddler's sensory enjoyment. Spread on a cookie sheet to dry. Or if you like, you can continue using white rice or white coarse salt. You will get many ideas of what to add to your bin from any of the picture books about

yellow. For example from the book <u>Yellow: Seeing Yellow All Around Us</u>, you could add any of the following items: sunflowers, plastic bee, lemons, plastic fried egg, plastic banana, rain hat, hard hat, flashlight, and chicks. Other suggestions for yellow items are: feathers, pompoms, buttons, pipe cleaners, toy cars, building blocks, plastic corn, glass stones.

SUPPLEMENTARY ACTIVITY:
Make a sparkling yellow bottle. You need an empty plastic water bottle or Gatorade bottle and add 1/2 cup clear corn syrup, yellow glitter or sequins. Turn the bottle on its side, slowly rotate it so that you evenly coat the sides with the corn syrup and glitter. Your toddler will enjoy watching the glitter slowly slip down the sides of the bottle. Show him how to turn the bottle on its side and rotate it.

Check out these videos on YouTube.com:

Grandma's Got A Little Yellow Car:
https://www.youtube.com/watch?v=YrDQt63I5wQ

The Color Yellow:
https://www.youtube.com/watch?v=4g4Ip4n1PhA

SNACK:

Show your child how to peel a banana by making a small cut for him and then ask him to pull down the peel. Place the banana on a cutting board and give your child a plastic knife. Show him how to slice the banana into chunks. Ask him to put the banana into your blender. Then add the following to make a Banana Smoothie: 1/2 cup milk, 1 tsp Vanilla, and several ice cubes.

MIXED COLORS

Life is about using the whole box of crayons.

- RuPaul

BOOKS TO READ:
My Little Colors Book by Roger Priddy
Red Green Blue: A First Book of Colors by Alison Jay
What Does Bunny See? A Book of Colors and Flowers by Linda Sue Park
And To Name But Just a Few: Red, Yellow, Green and Blue by Laurie Rosenwald
Mouse Paint by Ellen Stoll Walsh
Is It Red? Is It Yellow? Is It Blue? by Tana Hoban
Red, Blue, Yellow Shoe by Tana Hoban

SENSORY BIN:
Make a multi-colored pasta bin. Take some cooked pasta, make sure it is not overcooked. In 4 plastic bags, place a different color of food coloring such as red, blue, green and

yellow. Add 2 Tbsp of water to each bag and then add about 20 drops of food coloring. Divide the cooked pasta evenly between bags. Seal each bag and begin mixing the food color and pasta. Give one of the bags to your toddler to mix. Pour all the pasta into a large bowl and give your toddler tongs and a plastic pasta claw. Give her four containers and after her own tactile explorations, encourage her to sort some of the pasta by color.

SUPPLEMENTARY ACTIVITY:

Fill an ice cube tray with water. In each cube, add red, yellow, green or blue food coloring. Freeze. After the water is frozen, take out the cubes and put in a bowl of water. Give your child a large spoon or ladle to play with the ice cubes. See if she can scoop up the color that you request. If she wants to play with the ice cubes with her hands, just give her some mittens to wear.

Check out these videos on YouTube.com:

Eggy's Colorful Pants:
http://www.youtube.com/watch?v=XIAZULxRUFc

Colors Song:
http://www.youtube.com/watch/v=_9gCUpVwqa8

SNACK:
Give your child a plate with an assortment of food that is either red, blue, green or yellow. Suggestions: strawberries, apples, bananas, blueberries, green grapes. Have her name the colors of the fruit. You could even ask her to put each color of fruit in individual muffin cup liners before she eats them. Of course, you could just serve her some multicolored pasta you reserved from your large sensory bin and add her favorite sauce.

PURPLE

This donut has purple in the middle, purple is a fruit.

- Homer Simpson

BOOKS TO READ:
Sally and the Purple Socks by Lisze Bechtold
Harold and the Purple Crayon by Crockett Johnson
Chicken, Pig, Cow and the Purple Problem by Ruth Ohi
Purple: Seeing Purple All Around Us by Sarah Schuette
My Violet Book by Kathy Knowles

SENSORY BINS:
Place a package of purple water beads in a large plastic bowl and then add the amount of water as instructed. They need to soak approximately 6 to 8 hours before the beads are ready. Be careful to drain off the excess water before you pour the beads into your child's sensory bin. Add several drops of

lavender oil into the beads for an additional fragrant experience. Be prepared that the beads are quite bouncy and can easily end up all over your floor.

Give your toddler scoops and containers to transfer the beads into them. Make sure you have a plastic cloth on the floor for easy pick up. After your child has finished his own play with these beads, ask him to take off his socks and let him walk on these beads for another special tactile experience.

These beads will give your toddler days of fun and when they begin to shrink, add more water to plump them back up to size. Your child will be happy to use only scoops and buckets to play with these beads.

If you have difficulty locating purple water beads in a store, they can be substituted for purple aquarium sand found at a pet store.

SUPPLEMENTARY ACTIVITY:
Squirt some shaving cream, about the size of a tennis ball, into a sealable, plastic bag. Then add some red finger paint and blue finger paint. Seal the bag well and let your toddler squish the three colors together to create the color purple. Squeeze the new color onto a sheet of paper for him to finger paint.

Check out these videos on YouTube.com:

Sesame Street - Savion reads, "The Purple King":
http://www.youtube.com/watch?v=LT0qNwAx1Ss

Purple People Eater from Kidsongs.com: Very Silly Songs:
http://www.youtube.com/watch?v=REHV8LERhPw

SNACK:
Make a fun drink called a Purple Cow. Blend together the following ingredients in a blender: 1/2 cup unsweetened grape juice,

1 cup milk, and 1 sliced banana.

PINK

Pink isn't just a color, it's an attitude!

- Miley Cyrus

BOOKS TO READ:
Pink: Seeing Pink All Around Us by Michael Dahl
Double Pink by Kate Feiffer
Little Pink Pup by Johanna Kerby
Pink Magic by Donna Jo Napoli

SENSORY BIN:
Shred pink construction paper and pink wrapping paper for your filler. Now add a selection of pink items. Be sure to include some interesting containers, gift bags, and baskets that your child can use to pour in some of the filler or to sort some of the pink items. Bury some pink items in the filler for your toddler to discover. See if she can find them using tongs or large tweezers. She may need your permission to scrunch and tear the

shredded paper. Add any of the following pink items: hair clips, ribbons, bows, pompoms, buttons, toys and any other items mentioned in the books you have read.

Review the section, "Learning Moments" for ideas on things to do with your toddler after she is finished with her own explorations.

SUPPLEMENTARY ACTIVITY:
Make some fragrant paint by stirring together 1/2 Tbsp of hot water to one package of pink Kool-Aid. Give your child a paint brush and paper to paint with his scented paint.

Check out this video on YouTube.com:

The Paint is Pink - Preschool Music Baby: https://www.youtube.com/watch?v=cyolmlXFBYY

SNACK:
Make a Pink Milkshake. Blend together the following ingredients: 1/2 cup strawberries, 1

tsp vanilla extract, 3/4 cup milk, and 1 cup vanilla ice cream. Blend well and then pour into two glasses. Drink from clear glasses so that your toddler can see her pink drink.

ORANGE

Orange is the happiest color.

- Frank Sinatra

BOOKS TO READ:
Mathilda and the Orange Balloon by Randall De Seve and Jen Corrace
Orange: Seeing Orange All Around Us by Sarah L Schuette
Orange by Mary Elizabeth Salzmann
My Orange Book by Kathy Knowles

SENSORY BIN:
Color some rice orange. (Recipe on Page 16) For fragrance, squeeze some fresh orange juice into the rice. Let dry. Add this orange rice into a container. Your toddler can enjoy holding the rice and letting it slip through his fingers. Your child may only need a colander, scoop and funnels. However, you could include some large orange buttons, pipe cleaners, plastic oranges, and any other orange

toys.

SUPPLEMENTARY ACTIVITY:
Cut an orange in half and show your child how to squeeze out the juice into a small bowl. Pour into a small glass for your child to drink.

Check out this video on YouTube.com:

The Color Orange:
https://www.youtube.com/watch?v=pYbSUm3fftA

SNACK:
You have many choices for an orange snack: Goldfish crackers, orange slices, carrots sticks, cubed cheddar cheese or a dish of orange sherbet!

RAINBOW COLORS

My heart leaps up when I behold a rainbow in the sky.

- William Wordsworth

BOOKS TO READ:
Planting a Rainbow by Lois Ehlert
Elmer and the Rainbow by David McKee
A Rainbow of My Own by Don Freeman
Duckie's Rainbow by Frances Barry

SENSORY BINS:
Buy a large box of Fruit Loops Cereal. Blend half of the cereal for a colorful "dirt". Add the Fruit Loops "dirt" on one side of the container and the whole Fruit Loops on the other side. Give your toddler a variety of colorful flowers to plant in small pots. Add a rainbow of candles that she can insert in the small pots as well. Be sure to provide a variety of scoops.

SUPPLEMENTARY ACTIVITY:

Give your toddler a small bowl of Fruit Loop Cereal and a pipe cleaner to make an edible bracelet. Show her how to slide the Fruit Loops onto the pipe cleaner and twist the ends together to slip it on her wrist. If you have an older toddler, you could show her the pattern for a rainbow: Red, Orange, Yellow, Green, Blue, Indigo, Violet.

Check out this video on YouTube.com:

In The Rainbow Song:
http://www.youtube.com/watch?v=mUWvv3n42og

SNACK:

Bake some cupcakes and ice them. Have your toddler help you by sprinkling rainbow sprinkles on top of the icing.

BROWN

The color brown, I realized, is anything but nondescript. It comes in as many hues as there are colors of earth, which is commonly presumed infinite.

- Barbara Kingsolver, Animal Dreams

BOOKS TO READ:
Brown Bear, Brown Bear, What Do You See? by Eric Carle
Moo Moo, Brown Cow by Jakki Wood
Brown Is A Beautiful Color by Jean Carey Bond
Seeing Brown All Around Us by Michael Dahl
Big Brown Bear's Up and Down Day by David McPhail

SENSORY BIN:
Mix together 8 cups flour, 1 cup baby oil. Add approximately 1/4 cup of cocoa powder for a fragrant brown color. Add the brown dough to your child's sensory bin. He will enjoy playing with this texture that is really soft and

malleable. It will be even more enjoyable as he will enjoy the soft scent of baby oil. Use scoops, silicone muffin liners, muffin tin and small sand toys. Add other small brown items such as feathers, large buttons, and plastic animals.

SUPPLEMENTARY ACTIVITY:
Make a Brown Bear Paper Plate Mask. The following web-site has a bear mask template for the book Brown Bear Brown Bear What Do You See?
http://www.craftjr.com/printable-animal-masks-bear-mask/bear-mask-colored-2/.

Print this mask on card stock paper so that it won't easily tear. Cut out the mask and glue on the back of the mask a craft stick for a handle. Encourage your child to hold the mask in front of his face and roar like a bear.

He may be happy to hold the mask when he does the appropriate motions to the following verse:

Brown Bear, Brown Bear Turn around.
Brown Bear, Brown Bear Touch the ground.
Brown Bear, Brown Bear Reach up high.
Brown Bear, Brown Bear Touch the sky.
Brown Bear, Brown Bear Bend down low.
Brown Bear, Brown Bear Touch your toe.

Check out this video on YouTube.com:

The Color Brown: http://www.youtube.com/watch/v=JLbs0V6S7Oo

SNACK:
Give your toddler a glass of chocolate milk or a dish of chocolate pudding. If you have more time, get her help making a Wacky Cake. He will enjoy making the three holes in the pan. If you don't have a recipe, check the following web-site: http://allrecipes.com/recipe/wacky-cake-viii/. After your cake has baked and cooled, ice the cake, and then ask your child to sprinkle brown sprinkles on the cake.

BLACK

Without black, no color has any depth. But if you mix black with everything suddenly there's shadow - no, not just shadow, but fullness. You've got to be willing to mix black into your palette if you want to create something that's real.

- Amy Grant

BOOKS TO READ:
Ten Black Dots by Donald Crews
Black Meets White by Justine Fontes and Geoff Waring
Black All Around by Patricia Hubbell
Black: Seeing Black All Around Us by Michael Dahl
Itsy Bitsy Spider by Iza Trapani

SENSORY BIN:
Pour into your sensory bin a bag of black bird seed. In one section of the bin, you could also add some black beans. Add any small black items such as: pompoms, pipe cleaners, plastic spiders, small boxes, buttons, plastic animals,

cars, rocks, and any black Halloween items.

SUPPLEMENTARY ACTIVITY:
Give your child a sheet of white paper and black paint. Then give her a selection of the following black items to dip into the paint and paint on her paper: pompom, pipe cleaner, plastic spider, button and rock.

Check out this video on YouTube.com:

Baa Baa Black Sheep:
http://www.youtube.com/watch?v=gBEHFFnV3RY

SNACK:
Give her a snack from the following suggestions: Blackberries, Blackberry Yogurt, or Black Tortilla Chips with black bean dip.

WHITE

White is not a mere absence of color; it is a shining and affirmative thing, as fierce as red, as definite as black. God paints in many colors; but He never paints so gorgeously, I had almost said so gaudily, as when He paints in white.

- Gilbert K Chesterton

BOOKS TO READ:
White: Seeing White All Around Us by Michael Dahl
Little White Rabbit: by Kevin Henkes
Little White Duck by Walt Whippo
Pete The Cat: I Love My White Shoes by Eric Litwin

SENSORY BIN:
Pour into a large bowl some white navy beans or Epsom Salts. Beside the bowl, place in a bucket white items such as pompoms, styrofoam balls, cotton balls, cars, glass rocks, and sea shells. Give him a variety of items to

use for scooping and sorting.

SUPPLEMENTARY ACTIVITY:

Place a sheet of wax paper or parchment paper and place in the microwave. Lay a bar of ivory soap on top of the paper. Microwave this bar of soap for about 2 minutes on High. You and your toddler will enjoy watching this bar of soap grow.

When it has fully expanded, put this large chunk of dried white soap into a bowl and let your toddler break the chunk into smaller pieces. Take these small pieces, add a little warm water, and begin beating this mixture together. You can use a spoon but it is easier with an electric beater.

This mixture can be used the same way you would for play dough. You can place some of the mixture into cookie cutters and let them dry for a few days. Push the soap mixture out of the cookie cutters and your toddler will have shaped soaps to use in the bath tub.

SNACK:
Give him a cupcake with white icing or a bowl of vanilla ice cream and give him some shredded coconut to sprinkle on top.

BLACK AND WHITE

There's something strange and powerful about black-and-white imagery.

- Stefan Kanfer

BOOKS TO READ:
Black On White by Tana Hoban
White On Black by Tana Hoban
Black Meets White by Justine Fontes
Bold and Bright: Black And White Animals by Dorothy Patent

SENSORY BIN:
Mix black birdseed or black beans with white rice. As a variation, you could create two rows in the container - one with black birdseed on one side and white rice on the other side. Include any black and white items such as pompoms, pipe cleaners, plastic spiders, plastic ants, buttons, rocks and animals. A plastic zebra would be perfect. Give her some items that she hasn't used lately for pouring

and sorting.

SUPPLEMENTARY ACTIVITY:
Mix together 3/4 cup white paint and 1/4 cup salt. Give her a paintbrush to paint this mixture on a sheet of black construction paper. Any remaining paint can be stored in a container with a lid for later use.

SNACK:
Give her any of these suggestions for a snack: Dip blackberries in yogurt, Black olives, and pieces of cauliflower dipped in Ranch Dressing; or black tortilla chips with Black Bean Dip.

KALEIDOSCOPE OF COLORS

Every time you shift to a different color or different hue you are creating interest. It's a subtle thing but it builds content.

- Clyde Aspevig

BOOKS TO READ:
Color Dance by Anna Jonas
Skippyjon Jones: Color Crazy by Judith Schachner
Mary Wore Her Red Dress and Henry Wore His Green Sneakers by Merle Peek
And To Name Just A Few: Red Yellow Green and Blue by Laurie Rosenwald
The Deep Blue Sea: A Book About Colors by Audrey Wood

SENSORY BIN:
Pour into your container a variety of fillers that you have been using from other bins: black beans, black bird seed, colored rice, colored pasta, etc. (Recipe on Page 16) Or you

could do something completely different and add into the bin a box of puzzle pieces. Choose a puzzle that has lots of colorful pieces. Beside the bin, give your toddler a container of some of the many items you added for each specific color bin. After his own discoveries, encourage him to sort some of the items by size and others by color. Include different colors of plastic eggs for scooping. Make sure he has colorful containers to use as he scoops things into them.

SUPPLEMENTARY ACTIVITY:
As you cut various lengths of masking tape, stick one end to the edge of a plastic container. Have your toddler take these lengths and place on a sheet of paper. Give your child a selection of paint colors to paint on this sheet. When the paint dries, take off the strips of masking tape. Your child could also add some colorful stickers. Talk about how wonderful it is that we have so many colors to enjoy.

Check out these videos on YouTube.com:

Learn Color Train - Learning Colors for kids:
https://www.youtube.com/watch?v=lu9K13M_sB8

Learn Colors by Matching, Learning Colors:
https://www.youtube.com/watch?v=_AK6T3g5oyU

The Butterfly Song:
https://www.youtube.com/watch?v=RPAZHVNVJp0

SNACK:
For a special treat, give your child a small dish of colorful candies such as M&Ms or Jelly Beans, or a dish of Fruit Loops Cereal. If you would like to give him healthier food, put on his plate a selection of colorful fruit.

CHAPTER 3:

SEASON SENSORY BINS

Your toddler has already experienced the changing seasons as a baby, but this is the first year that she will be more aware of what is happening. Your walks outside, your conversations and now her interactions with these seasonal bins will help your toddler to better comprehend how seasons change.

BEFORE YOU START THESE BINS:

1. For each season, there are three different types of sensory bins. Decide how you are going to introduce these

different aspects of each season. Will you give your toddler a bin each month of the specific season, or will you do all three bins at the beginning of each season? Alternatively, you might just choose one of the bins for each season and introduce all four seasons in one month.
2. Check out the list of specific books for each season and put on hold whatever your library has.
3. When you are planning a topic, can you take your toddler somewhere to help her better understand what you have been introducing? For example, when you do the apples bin, is it the right time of the year to see some apples growing on a tree? When you are doing the fishing bin, can you take him to a store and look at some fish and even some fishing gear? When you are doing the skating bin, can you take him somewhere to slip and slide on an ice skating rink?

FURTHER ENRICHMENT:

1. Choose some clothing that is appropriate for the season you are introducing and place in a suitcase. She will enjoy unpacking the suitcase and trying on the clothes. On another day, add clothing that is appropriate for two different seasons and ask her to sort the clothing.
2. Start a binder called Seasons. You will need 4 dividers, one for each season. As you do various activities for each season, include some of the artwork in this binder. Sheet protectors work well for storing these items. Also, include photos of your child dressed for each season.
3. Use play dough to teach the seasons:
    a. Find appropriate molds and cookie cutters for each season. For example, use flower molds for spring, leaves for autumn, and Christmas trees for Christmas.

b. Add essential oils or Kool-Aid or juice that are appropriate for each season: floral essential oils for spring, watermelon Kool-Aid for summer, apple for fall. Add spices to conjure up seasonal smells such as apple pie spice or pumpkin pie spice for autumn or cinnamon for winter.
c. Make imprints in the play dough with appropriate seasonal items.
d. Hide small seasonal items in a large clump of the play dough. Give him tweezers and a spoon to find them.
e. Give her a selection of seasonal items to add to her play dough to make a sculpture.
f. Go for walks and collect items that can be used in your seasonal play dough activities: rocks, twigs, leaves, flowers, and pinecones.
g. Print and laminate the play dough mats from the following

web-site for the various seasons: http://www.kidsparkz.com/playdough-mats.html
4. The following web-site provides printable paper dolls and appropriate clothing to teach the different seasons: http://www.makingfriends.com/friends/f_seasonal.htm

<u>WINTER</u>

Winter came down to our home one night

Quietly pirouetting in on silvery-toed slippers of snow,

And we, we were children once again.

- Bill Morgan, Jr.

SNOW

BOOKS TO READ:
The Snowy Day by Ezra Keats
In The Snow by Peggy Collins
It's Snowing by Gail Gibbons
Winter Snow by Liesbet Slegers
All You Need For A Snowman by Alice Schertle
Let's Look at Winter by Sarah Schuette

SENSORY BIN:
If you live where there is snow, fill up a large shallow container with snow. Use various sand molds to create shapes in the snow. Give your child some mittens to keep his hands warm. You could also show him how to make balls and create a snowman. Include some items to make a snowman such as large googly eyes, a small carrot for its nose, raisins for its mouth and buttons on its body.

If you don't have access to real snow, you can buy instant snow online at http://www.stevespanglerscience.com/product/instant-snow

SUPPLEMENTARY ACTIVITY:
Add a different color of paint on several paper plates. Set out a large sheet of paper for painting. Put a mitten on one of your child's hands and tell him he can press that hand onto the paint and then "paint" on the sheet of paper. Your toddler can also sprinkle some glitter on his painting.

SNACK:
Put two scoops of vanilla ice cream on top of each other and put in another dish an assortment of food items that can be added to your snowman: pieces of banana, raisins, M&M's, cherries, and perhaps a large strawberry for its hat. Help your child put them on the ice cream before it begins to melt!

If you have real snow, collect some freshly fallen snow and put some in a bowl. Pour some maple syrup or some frozen juice concentrate on top and you have a special snow cone.

ICE SKATING

BOOKS TO READ:
Skating Day by Mercer Mayer
Skating With The Bears by Andrew Breakspeare
Callie Cat, Ice Skater by Eileen Spinelli
Dream Big, Little Pig! by Kristi Yamaguchi
Skating by Donna Bailey

SENSORY BIN:
Fill a shallow container with water and add some plastic fish at the bottom. Freeze this container to make a "skating rink". If you have any appropriate Christmas decorations such as Christmas Village Trees, place them on the rink. Add a few pinecones. Then give your child various small toys and small figurines to play on the rink. Add some large pieces of building blocks like Duplo. Your child will enjoy seeing how everything slides across the ice. As the ice melts, tell your toddler she is going to ice fish. Give her

spoons to begin cracking the ice to see if she can catch a fish with an aquarium net or scoop.

SUPPLEMENTARY ACTIVITY:
Fill an ice cube tray with water. In two of the cubes, add two different colors of food coloring. Let it partially freeze and then add two craft sticks into those two colored cubes. When the ice is completely frozen, give your child a sheet of paper and let her paint with her colored ice cubes.

SNACK:
After skating outside, it is always enjoyable to have some hot chocolate. To make it extra special, make your toddler some hot chocolate and add some miniature marshmallows. Of course, don't serve it to your toddler too hot!

WINTER ANIMALS

BOOKS TO READ:
Over and Under The Snow by Kate Messner
When Winter Comes by Nancy Van Laan
A Little Bit Of Winter by Paul Stewart
Bedtime For Bear by Brett Helquist
Sleep Big Bear, Sleep! by Maureen Wright
When Snowflakes Fall by Carl Sams
Animals In Winter by Henrietta Bancroft
Under The Snow by Melissa Stewart

SENSORY BIN:
Fill the container with the following: white rice, white pompoms, white cotton balls, glass gems, plastic spruce trees (that you may have from any Christmas Villages), and a small box for a cave. Set some plastic animals you have in a small container and explain that these animals must go to sleep for the winter. You will need a variety of animals: bears, badgers, spiders, bats, chipmunks, squirrels, hedgehogs, raccoons, and skunks. Some sleep

in trees, some burrow down into the snow and others sleep in caves. Suggest that she tucks the animals into bed for the winter. Encourage him to use his shovel or small scoops to move the materials around in the smaller container to find good homes for the animals.

SUPPLEMENTARY ACTIVITY:

Create a bear cave by placing a blanket over a table so that your toddler can go under the table. You may want to put some comfortable pillows or blanket on the floor. Explain that many winter animals like to sleep at least some of the winter. This could be a great location to read about winter animals.

SNACK:

Give your child some Teddy Grahams or some gummy bears. Or give your toddler a selection of berries and explain that bears eat them before they go and hibernate.

SPRING

Spring is nature's way of saying, "Let's party!"

- Robin Williams

CHICKS AND EGGS

BOOKS TO READ:
Everything Spring by Jill Esbaum
Dora's Chicks by Julie Sykes
Whose Chick Are You? by Nancy Tafuri
Let's Look at Spring by Sarah Schuette
Wee Little Chick by Lauren Thompson

SENSORY BIN:
Color some rice yellow or green and add some lemon juice to the rice for added fragrance. (Recipe on Page 16) Add small bunny rabbits, chicks, and plastic eggs. Include a basket or container to collect the eggs. You could also add some Easter grass in the container to make a home for the baby chicks.

SUPPLEMENTARY ACTIVITY:
You will need 6 boiled eggs, a plastic hammer, a picture of an egg or a chick, glue and food coloring. Take out three containers and fill

with water. Add a different food coloring to each one. Place some egg shells in each container making sure that the egg shells are completely immersed. After you have dyed the eggs, let them dry. Then place the shells into a plastic bag, seal it and give it to your toddler. Give her a plastic hammer to smash the egg shells.

Take a sheet of paper and draw a large Easter egg or a chick. If you need a template, print one from the following website: http://www.craftjr.com/easter-templates/.

Spread glue inside the picture. Place the picture on a cookie sheet to help contain the mess. Show your toddler how to sprinkle some of the egg shells over the glue. If your child does not like the texture of the egg shells, put some thin mittens on her. When the glue dries, shake off the extra loose shells. Your child could also add some glitter glue.

Check out this video on YouTube.com:

Chick Hatching:
https://www.youtube.com/watch?v=tof5b1Qs_OE

SNACK:
Make some egg salad sandwiches from the eggs you boiled earlier.

CATERPILLARS AND BUTTERFLIES

BOOKS TO READ:
So Many Butterflies! by Lara Bergen
Olivia and the Butterfly Adventure by Natalie Shaw
My, Oh My - A Butterfly by Tish Rabe
Bob and Otto by Robert Bruel
Follow Me Mittens by Lola Schaefer
The Very Hungry Caterpillar by Eric Carle

SENSORY BIN:
Pour some green split peas into the container. Add plastic caterpillars and butterflies, butterfly nets, bug jars, twigs, leaves, and a magnifying glass. If you can't find plastic caterpillars, glue together three small pompoms. Make sure you explain that caterpillars turn into butterflies.

SUPPLEMENTARY ACTIVITY:
Check out the following web-site for butterfly templates: http://www.activityvillage.co.uk/butterfly_printables.htm. Print and cut out one of the butterflies, and give your child a variety of items to decorate his butterfly: paint, stickers, ribbons and glitter glue.

Check out these videos on YouTube.com:

Time-lapse of Butterfly Lifecycle: http://www.youtube.com/watch?v=cAUSKxWMIh0

Butterfly Colors Song: http://www.youtube.com/watch?v=RPAZHVNVJp0

SNACK:
Fill a plastic snack bag with yogurt raisins and dried cranberries or any other snack food.
 Give your toddler a wooden clothes peg and some glitter glue to spread on one side of the clothes peg. You can also add two googly eyes. Attach the dried clothes peg to the

middle of the bag. If you like, cut a pipe cleaner around 5 inches long. Bend the piece in half and clip on the clothes peg for the butterfly's antennae.

Sensory Play

SPRING RAIN

BOOKS TO READ:
Here Comes The Rain by Mary Murphy
In the Rain with Baby Duck by Amy Hest
It's Raining, It's Pouring by Kim Eagle
Listen To The Rain by Bill Martin Jr & John Archambault
Peter Spier's Rain by Peter Spier
Who Is Tapping At My Window? by A. G. Deming

SENSORY BIN:
Add a large floral craft foam to the bin and a variety of artificial spring flowers such as tulips. Provide a small container of water and include colanders, strainers, large eye droppers, and a child's watering can.

SUPPLEMENTARY ACTIVITY:
Give your toddler a sheet of white paper and markers and have her color on the paper. Go

outside, put the picture on a table in the rain and then go back inside. Have her watch the rain fall on her picture and see how the colors slowly start to run together. Return outside and bring the wet picture inside to dry.

If it is raining too hard, she can just watch as the colors run together and get completely washed away by the rain. She may want to color several sheets of paper to continue taking them outside to be rained upon! If it isn't raining, do the same activity, but give her a squirt bottle filled with water and she can provide the "rain."

SNACK:
Decorate cupcakes by inserting small paper umbrellas in each one. If you have umbrellas left over, use them for an activity of sorting them by color.

SUMMER

Summer afternoon, summer afternoon; to me those have always been the two most beautiful words in the English language.

- Henry James

Gayle Jervis & Kristen Jervis Cacka

GONE FISHING

BOOKS TO READ:
That's Papa's Way by Kate Banks
Little Shark by Anne Rockwell
Fishing: A Mr. and Mrs. Green Adventure by Keith Baker
Stanley Goes Fishing by Craig Frazier
Loudmouth George and the Fishing Trip by Nancy L. Carson
Piggy and Dad Go Fishing by David Martin
Hooray For Fish by Lucy Cousins

SENSORY BIN:
Fill an outdoor child's water table or a large container with water. Add some water beads or aquarium rocks and toss into the water some plastic fish. Give your child a small fish net that can be bought at any pet store. Also, your child will need a bucket to store the fish he has caught. For a variation, freeze a few plastic fish in a small container of water and then add to the pool. He will enjoy watching

the ice slowly melt so that he can retrieve the fish.

SUPPLEMENTARY ACTIVITY:
Fill some balloons partially full of water and then tie knots on the balloons. Toss them into a wading pool for play, pretending they are sharks.

Take your toddler to a pet store to look at some fish. You may even want to buy him a gold fish or a beta fish when you are there!

SNACK:
Make some Tuna Fish Sandwiches and give him some Gold Fish Crackers. Or make blue Jello and as it thickens, add some gummy fish.

SEASHELLS BY THE SEASHORE

BOOKS TO READ:
Can You Hear The Sea? by Judy Cumberbatch
Biscuit's First Beach Day by Alyssa S. Capucilli
On The Seashore by Anna Milbourne
Water Sings Blue: Ocean Poems by Kate Coombs
All You Need For A Beach by Alice Schertle

SENSORY BIN:
Fill a large container with sand and seashells and fill another container with water. Your child can enjoy collecting the seashells and putting them back into the water. Give her a magnifying glass to look more closely at the seashells. She may enjoy using tongs, a shovel, and a bucket to collect the seashells. Give her a sponge to wash the sea shells that she retrieves from the sand.

SUPPLEMENTARY ACTIVITY:

Give your child some paint, a sheet of paper and some seashells. Dip the seashells into various colors of paint and stamp their imprints onto the paper.

SNACK:

Cook some shell pasta and serve with your child's favorite sauce. You could also boil for about ten minutes some of the seashells your toddler was playing with to make sure they are clean. Then serve some fruit on the seashells.

BOAT RIDES

BOOKS TO READ:
Big Dog and Little Dog Go Sailing by Selina Young
Boat Book by Gail Gibbons
The Little Sailboat by Lois Lenski
Sail Away by Donald Crews
Boats: Speeding! Sailing! Cruising! by Patricia Hubbell

SENSORY BIN:
Collect various plastic boats from your child's toys and from the Dollar Store. Fill a small wading pool or shallow container with water and then add the boats. Give your child a straw to blow on a boat to see if he can make it go faster. Give him a bucket filled with some of the following items to add to the water and to the boats: small glass rocks, pebbles, seashells, plastic ocean creatures, and toy people to put in the boats.

SUPPLEMENTARY ACTIVITY:

Print the following activity where your child matches the color of the sail to the appropriate sailboat:
http://www.kidsparkz.com/boats-matching-games.html

Make a variety of boats with plastic, styrofoam and foil containers. Add some play dough to the bottoms, a mast from a twig or bamboo skewer and a sail from construction paper or flannel.

SNACK:

Make deviled eggs. Cut out red and green peppers in the shape of a triangle for their sails. If your toddler doesn't like peppers, just cut out a triangle from construction paper and stick through a tooth pick and insert into the eggs.

FALL

Autumn is a second spring when every leaf is a flower.

- Albert Camus

COLORFUL LEAVES

BOOKS TO READ:
Leaves Fall Down by Lisa Bullard
The Leaves on the Trees by Thom Wiley
Fall Leaves by Martha Rustad
Who Loves the Fall by Bob Raczka
Let It Fall by Maryann Cocca-Leffler
It's Fall by Linda Glaser
Fall Leaves Fall! by Zoe Hall

SENSORY BIN:
Collect a large bag filled with leaves. If it is a warm fall day, fill a container outside with all of your leaves. Let your toddler have fun crushing them, scooping them into other containers, and even sorting them by size and color. If you have any pinecones, hide them in the leaves for your toddler to find. Also, you could hide some plastic apples or small pumpkins.

If you are not doing this bin during the fall, or do not live where you see leaves change color, buy some fall leaves at the Dollar Store or at a Craft Store.

SUPPLEMENTARY ACTIVITY:
Place several leaves under a sheet of paper. Tape the paper onto the surface. Then show your child how to use her crayon to color over the leaves and create a picture of leaves.

Check out these videos on YouTube.com:

Falling Leaves - Nursery Rhyme:
http://www.youtube.com/watch?v=uu4ojfxOFXQ

Classic Sesame Street Animation - Leaves:
http://www.youtube.com/watch?v=mpzC8wZQuVM

Silly Bus - Leaves:
http://www.youtube.com/watch?v=Lq_3NPGz_Ic

SNACK:

Create a leaf shape from several slices of bread. When you have these leaf shapes, place them on a cookie sheet and toast in the oven for a few minutes. Then give your toddler several colors of jam such as Grape, Strawberry and Peach to color her leaves.

APPLES

BOOKS TO READ:
Applesauce Season by Eden Ross Lipson
Dappled Apples by Jan Carr
Eating Apples by Gail Saunders-Smith
Fall Apples by Martha Rustad
Ten Red Apples by Pat Hutchins
Ten Apples Up On Top by Theo LeSieg
The Apple Pie Tree by Zoe Hall
From Seed To Apple by Anita Ganeri

SENSORY BINS:
Pour some green split peas into your bin. Then add the following items: pinecones, acorns, plastic red and green apples, green split peas, 2 small pails, and a small truck. Provide tongs and a bucket or basket for your child to collect the apples.

SUPPLEMENTARY ACTIVITY:
Take a close look at an apple and identify its various parts: apple's skin, stem, flesh, core and seeds. You could even buy red and green apples to explain that there are different kinds of apples. Cut a piece of apple from both types for your child to taste.

Take half of an apple and pour some red paint on a paper plate. Show your child how to make apple prints on a sheet of paper.

Check out this video on YouTube.com:

I Like Apples Song:
http://www.youtube.com/watch?v=wTTz2dL0jb8

SNACK:
Give your child some sliced apples and yogurt for dip. An alternative snack is to give your child a dish of applesauce.

PUMPKINS

BOOKS TO READ:
Fall Pumpkins by Martha Rustad
It's Pumpkin Day, Mouse! by Laura Joffe Numeroff
From Seed to Pumpkin by Wendy Pfeiffer

SENSORY BIN:
Buy a pumpkin, cut off its top and place the pumpkin in a container. Let your child enjoy scooping out the seeds. This bin is very simple to do, but it could be rather messy. As always, surround your bin with a plastic cloth.

If your child doesn't like the texture of scooping out the pumpkin seeds and pulp, give him a light pair of mittens to wear.

SUPPLEMENTARY ACTIVITY:
Make the following play dough recipe for your toddler to make pretend loaves, pies,

muffins and cookies. A recipe is included below:

    5 cups Water
    2½ cups Salt
    3 Tbsp. Cream of Tartar
    10 Tbsp. Vegetable Oil
    5 cups Flour
    4 tsp Pumpkin Pie Spice
    1 tsp Cinnamon

Mix all the ingredients together in a large pot over low heat and stir frequently until the dough becomes quite thick and sticky. Then add some orange food coloring (combine red and yellow drops if you don't have orange) to the mixture and knead the dough. When it has cooled, the dough is ready for use.

Set out all the necessary baking supplies including the appropriate baking dishes and such items as a child's rolling pin, cookie sprinkles, cookie scoop or ice cream scoop, and pumpkin cookie cutters. If your child has a play kitchen, he may decide to bake his creations.

SNACK:

Serve your child a slice of pumpkin pie and have your child add some cool whip or ice cream on his piece of pie.

Take the pumpkin seeds that your toddler pulled out of the pumpkin, wash them and dry on a cookie sheet. Bake them at 350 F until brown. Salt, cool and eat.

CHAPTER 4: CELEBRATION SENSORY BINS

Every month, there is at least one day that has a special celebration. While your toddler may not understand the significance of each occasion, she can appreciate that the day is different from other days, that the day includes special items or includes special food and activities.

BEFORE YOU START THESE BINS:

A celebration for each month has been included. However, notice that Easter has been placed in April even though some years, it can be in March. In July, we have included both Canada Day and Independence Day. This provides a great opportunity to introduce another country to your toddler. You will also notice that there are two celebrations for Thanksgiving, one for Canada in October and one for United States in November. Since there isn't really an official celebration in August, we have included a Birthday Sensory Bin for that month. However, you may decide to use this bin in the month of your child's own birthday.

1. Reserve the books early at the library since there is often a demand for these types of books as you get closer to the time of the celebration.
2. Consider what traditions you and your family may want to start with each new celebration. You will get some great ideas from the following book: <u>The Book of New Family Traditions: How to Create Great Rituals for Holidays and Every Day</u> by Meg Cox.

FURTHER ENRICHMENT:

1. Use play dough to help him enjoy these various celebrations:
    a. Find appropriate molds and cookie cutters for each celebration. For example, use hearts for Valentine's Day, shamrocks for St. Patrick's Day, and crosses for Easter.
    b. Make imprints in the play dough with appropriate items for each celebration.
    c. Make play dough appropriate for the celebration. For example, make Chocolate Play Dough by adding some cocoa to your play dough recipe for Valentine's Day. Add green glitter to your green play dough for St. Patrick's Day.
    d. Add essential oils, bath oils, massage oils, and other fragrances to your play dough. For instance, add some floral essential oil or scented bath oil

for Mother's Day.

   e. Hide some objects in a clump of play dough that reflect the celebration. Give her large tweezers and a spoon to find them.

2. The following website has some great play dough mats that you can print on card stock and laminate or put between contact paper. They have mats for the following celebrations: Chinese New Year, Easter, Halloween, and Christmas. http://www.kidsparkz.com/playdough-mats.html

3. Dress your child in appropriate clothing for each celebration. You will most likely find some fun items at the Dollar Store including hats and necklaces. Choose particular colors that reflect the celebration such as red for Chinese New Year's Day and Valentine's Day, and green for St. Patrick's Day.

JANUARY: CHINESE NEW YEAR

Wishing you health, wealth and longevity this Chinese New Year

BOOKS TO READ:
Bringing In The New Year by Grace Lin
D Is For Dragon Dance by Ying Chang Compestine
Dragon Dance by Joan Holub
Lanterns and Firecrackers: A Chinese New Year Story by Jonny Zucker
My First Chinese New Year by Karen Katz

SENSORY BIN:
Place three containers with rice, soy beans and chow mein noodles into your long shallow bin. In the remaining space of the large bin, add any of the following: a small globe, fan (folded pleats on a pretty piece of paper, tied with pipe cleaner), gold fish or other plastic fish, panda bear, fortune cookies, dragon, lion, red envelopes stuffed with chocolate coins, several Christmas crackers, blossoms, and

small "take out" boxes. Give your child tongs, a scoop and large tweezers to help with his explorations.

SUPPLEMENTARY ACTIVITY:
Check out the following website for coloring pages regarding Chinese New Year:
http://www.sparklebox.co.uk/3631-3640/sb3637.html

Check out this video on YouTube.com:

Chinese New Year Song:
http://www.youtube.com/watch?v=BnJhOUyR204

SNACK:
Get your toddler's help to make Chow Mein Clusters. The recipe is below. He will also enjoy taking apart fortune cookies to discover something inside it.

Chow Mein Clusters:

Melt one 12 oz package of chocolate chips in the microwave or on the stove. Add a package of chow mein noodles and mix until evenly coated with the chocolate mixture.

Put parchment paper on two cookie sheets and then drop clusters of this mixture on the cookie sheets. Let them cool and set. If you like, you can add a few M & M candies or Smarties on top.

FEBRUARY: VALENTINE'S DAY

*I claim there ain't
Another saint
As great as Valentine.*
- Ogden Nash

BOOKS TO READ:
The Story of Valentine's Day by Nancy Skarmeas
Clifford's First Valentine's Day by Norman Bridwell
Little Bear's Valentine by Else H. Minari
Be Mine, Be Mine, Sweet Valentine by Sarah Weeks
Where Is Baby's Valentine by Karen Katz

SENSORY BIN:
Fill your bin with red or pink colored rice. (Recipe on Page 16) Add specific Valentine's Day items such as the following: heart shaped muffin tins, heart shaped erasers, rose petals, flowers, red pompoms and a heart-shaped ice cube tray.

SUPPLEMENTARY ACTIVITY:
Make some Chocolate Play Dough for your toddler to do some pretend baking. Then give your child the following items: cookie sheet, cookie scoop, Valentine cookie cutters, and Valentine cupcake liners or muffin tin.

An empty box of chocolates that has the chocolate insert, works well for holding pretend candies. Give her a container of baking sprinkles to sprinkle on top of her baking.

Chocolate Play Dough

Stir the following ingredients together in a saucepan over a low heat:

> 4 cups Water
> 3 1/4 cups Flour
> 3/4 cup Cocoa
> 2 cups Salt
> 4 Tbsp Vegetable Oil
> 3 Tbsp Cream of Tartar

When the dough begins to form, let it cool.

SNACK:

Make heart-shaped grilled cheese sandwiches or a Nutella Sandwich.

Cut several slices of bread into heart shapes and recruit your child's help to spread some red jam on top of the bread.

You can also give him Valentine's Day cookies. If you make the cookies yourself, get your toddler's help when adding sprinkles.

MARCH: ST. PATRICK'S DAY

An Irish Blessing

May love and laughter light your days, and warm your heart and home. May good and faithful friends be yours, wherever you may roam. May peace and plenty bless your world with joy that long endures. May all life's passing seasons bring the best to you and yours!

BOOKS TO READ:
St. Patrick's Day by Brenda Haugen
The Story of St. Patrick's Day by Patricia Pingry
Green Shamrocks by Eve Bunting
Jeremy Bean's St. Patrick's Day by Alice Schertle

SENSORY BIN:
Use anything green as your base such as green split peas, green colored rice or green colored pasta. (Recipe on Page 16) Then add items for your child to sort, measure and examine such as shamrocks, green pompoms, plastic shamrock necklace that you could keep intact

or break into pieces, plastic gold coins or green shamrock coins. You may also find at the Dollar Store shamrock shot glasses and cups to use for containers.

SUPPLEMENTARY ACTIVITY:
Dress your child in something green and give her some items to wear such as a leprechaun hat, shamrock pin, or shamrock necklace.

Take some of the items from your sensory bin that could be used to make a collage: paper shamrocks, pieces of the shamrock necklace, pompoms, or any green filler. Spread glue on a sheet of firm card stock paper or on a thin piece of cardboard. Have your toddler add the items on the glued surface.

SNACK:
If you have shamrock shape cookie cutters, bake some cookies and get your child's help to frost them with green icing and green sprinkles.

Get your child's help to make a "Shamrock Shake." Blend 1 cup of milk, 1 cup lime sherbet, and 1 banana.

Serve your child a scoop of vanilla ice cream, add a few drops of natural green food coloring, and have him mix it together. She will enjoy watching her ice cream turn green.

APRIL: EASTER

Do not abandon yourselves to despair. We are the Easter people and hallelujah is our song.

- Pope John Paul II

BOOKS TO READ:
Berenstain Bears and The Easter Story by Jan Berenstain
On That Easter Morning by Mary Joslin
The Story of Easter by Lucia Fisher
The Berenstain Bears and the Real Easter Eggs by Stan Berenstain

SENSORY BIN:
For your filler, add some Easter grass. Add large plastic eggs that she can put other smaller Easter items into such as small chicks or erasers. Add a variety of Easter related items such as a decorative bird's nest, small plastic eggs and Easter baskets. Choose some Easter items that can be inserted into a floral foam or an empty parmesan container. Insert

small items into the plastic eggs for his discovery. Also, put some items in the eggs that create different sounds such as grains of rice, some dried beans, and some buttons.

SUPPLEMENTARY ACTIVITY:
Play a matching game with Easter stickers. Buy Easter Stickers making sure there are at least doubles of each sticker. Place one sticker on a plastic egg and then its match on another egg. Place them in two different baskets. Continue doing this with a variety of stickers. Now have your toddler find the matching eggs.

Paint six craft sticks brown. When they are dry, glue two of them together to form a cross. Repeat with the remaining craft sticks. Fill a small plant pot with Easter grass, and then insert the three crosses into the pot.

SNACK:
Place half of each plastic egg into an egg

container. Then fill them with tasty snacks, such as raisins, carrot sticks, sliced strawberries, grapes, small pieces of cheese, etc.

MAY: MOTHER'S DAY

Motherhood: All love begins and ends there.

- Robert Browning

BOOKS TO READ:
Mother's Day by Anne Rockwell
The Berenstain Bears: We Love Our Mom by Jan Berenstain
Berenstain Bears and the Mama's Day Surprise by Stan Berenstain
The Mother's Day Mice by Eve Bunting
The Night Before Mother's Day by Natasha Wing

SENSORY BIN:
Fill a large bowl with brightly colored pompoms and white cotton balls. Then place this bowl into a larger container that will hold a variety of Mother's Day items: bath bombs, flowers, plastic vase, hair curlers, purse, lip gloss, necklace, index cards sprayed with colognes, fragrant candles, buttons, jewelry

boxes, anything that has bling, bracelets, items from Valentine's Day, flowers, and small, colorful containers.

SUPPLEMENTARY ACTIVITY:
Pretend that you and your toddler are going to a spa. Both of you can enjoy the sensation of two cool cucumbers placed on your eyes as you lie down and listen to some quiet music. Soak your feet in some warm water with some of the bath salts she helped make. Your toddler will enjoy rubbing lotion on his legs and feet while you do the same. Paint his toe nails or place temporary tattoos on his legs.

SNACK:
Plan a Teddy Bear Tea Party. Both you and your toddler could dress up for the tea as well as arrange all of your child's dolls and teddy bears on a blanket. Set up your child's plates and tea cups for the teddies and dolls. Lay out two place settings for you and your toddler. Serve iced tea and biscuits.

JUNE: FATHER'S DAY

It is a wise father that knows his own child.

- William Shakespeare

BOOKS TO READ:
Father's Day by Anne Rockwell
Happy Father's Day by Mercer Mayer
A Perfect Father's Day by Eve Bunting
Berenstain Bears and the Papa's Day Surprise by Stan Berenstain

SENSORY BIN:
On one side of a large container, place a bowl of coffee beans along with two small containers and some measuring spoons. On the other side of the large container, add the following items: golf tees, a chunk of floral foam wrapped in a brown paper bag and a plastic hammer. She can use her hammer to 'pound' the golf tees into the floral foam 'wood'.

SUPPLEMENTARY ACTIVITY:
Talk to your toddler about what his Dad likes to wear. Does he wear sports shirts? Golf shirts? Baseball caps? Ties to work? Find something appropriate for your toddler to wear that his dad would wear.

Give your child a pipe cleaner and some large washers. Show her how to slip them onto the pipe cleaner.

Give her some large nuts and bolts to take apart and put back together.

SNACK:
Have a picnic outside and eat some watermelon. If it is too cold for a picnic, place a blanket on the floor and have an indoor picnic.

JULY: CANADA DAY

I am a Canadian, free to speak without fear, free to worship in my own way, free to stand for what I think right, free to oppose what I believe wrong, or free to choose those who shall govern my country. This heritage of freedom I pledge to uphold for myself and all mankind.

- John Diefenbaker (Canadian Bill of Rights, July 1, 1960)

BOOKS TO READ:
Good Night Canada by Adam Gamble
Hey Freddy It's Canada's Birthday by Susan Chalker Browne
Out On The Prairie by Cora Taylor
Canada 123 by Per-Henrik Gurth

SENSORY BIN:
Pour into your sensory bin some red rice on each side and then in the middle, add some white rice. (Recipe on Page 16) Explain to your toddler that Canada's colors are red and

white. Add red and white items such as buttons, pompoms, and pipe cleaners. Include all sorts of Canadian souvenir items such as: Canadian flag, maple leaf, keychain, pencils, erasers, map of Canada, a small globe, hockey player figurine, plastic hockey puck, beaver, moose, etc. You could even hide some Canadian coins in the rice.

SUPPLEMENTARY ACTIVITY:
Show your child some Canadian coins, and then place the coins under a sheet of paper. Tape down the sheet of paper and give her some crayons to make some coin rubs. Check out the following website for all sorts of crafts for Canada Day: http://www.dltk-kids.com/canada/

Check out this video on YouTube.com:

Oh Canada Anthem: http://www.youtube.com/watch?v=ZOY0-MBOh_o

SNACK:

Make some pancakes and have some maple syrup. Explain how we get maple syrup from big maple trees that grow in parts of Canada.

A simple dessert for your toddler to help you make is filling a clear glass dish with strawberries, then yogurt, and finally strawberries. Insert a candle and sing "Happy Birthday to Canada."

JULY: INDEPENDENCE DAY

And I'm proud to be an American,
Where at least I know I'm free.
And I won't forget the men who died,
who gave that right to me.

- Lee Greenwood

BOOKS TO READ:
Grandma Drove The Garbage Truck by Katie Clark
Apple Pie 4th of July by Janet Wong

SENSORY BIN:
Pour into your sensory bin some red rice on one side, white in the middle, and some blue rice on the other side (Recipe on Page 16) Explain that American colors are red, white and blue. Add all sorts of American souvenir items such as: flag, keychain, pencils, erasers, a small globe, bell, eagle, coins, etc. Add any other items that are red, white or blue such as pompoms, buttons, and pipe cleaners.

SUPPLEMENTARY ACTIVITY:
Show your child some American coins, and then place the coins under a sheet of paper. Tape down the sheet of paper and give him some crayons to make some coin rubs.

If you have a Smart Phone, check out the Fireworks App and let your toddler enjoy seeing some fireworks.

Check out the following web-site for all sorts of crafts for Independence Day:
http://www.dltk-kids.com/usa/

SNACK:
Mix in layers of vanilla yogurt, strawberries and blueberries. Make sure you give your toddler a clear glass dish so that he can see the colors.

AUGUST: BIRTHDAYS

And in the end, it's not the years in your life that count. It's the life in your years.

- Abraham Lincoln

BOOKS TO READ:
Birthdays by Rosemary Wells
How Do Dinosaurs Say Happy Birthday? by Jane Yolen
Happy Birthday, Little Pookie by Sandra Boynton
A Birthday for Bear by Bonny Becker
Otis & Sydney and the Best Birthday Ever by Laura Joffe Numeroff

SENSORY BIN:
Put multicolored pasta in your bin. (Recipe on Page 16) Add ribbons, bows, gift bags, party hats, noisemakers, paper cups, paper plates, candles, and party favors. Include any cupcake play food, cupcake holders, plastic measuring cup, measuring spoon and any scoops. Also,

add a floral foam to insert candles.

SUPPLEMENTARY ACTIVITY:
Tear some birthday wrapping paper into small pieces to make a collage. Give your child this paper, some ribbons and bows and a firm paper plate. Put glue on the whole plate and have her place these small items wherever she chooses. Then give her some glitter glue and birthday stickers to add to her collage.

SNACK:
Decorate a cupcake with icing and sprinkles. Insert a candle, light it and sing "Happy Birthday to You," and then blow out the candle.

SEPTEMBER: BACK TO SCHOOL

You can teach a student a lesson for a day; but if you can teach him to learn by creating curiosity, he will continue the learning process as long as he lives.

- Clay Bedford

BOOKS TO READ:
Marco Goes to School by Roz Chast
Seven Little Mice Go To School by Haruo Yamashita
First Day of School by Anne Rockwell
Back to School Tortoise by Lucy M George
This School Year Will Be The Best! by Kay Winters

SENSORY BIN:
Take some used paper and shred it for your filler. Add any items that are school related for your child's exploration and enjoyment: alphabet blocks, calculator, pencils and erasers, numbers, large paper clips, small dry erase board or chalk board, dry erase markers

or chalk, pencil case, pencil holders, small journal book, post-it notes, and lunch box with some play food. Remember to include any additional containers for sorting plus scoops for the filler.

SUPPLEMENTARY ACTIVITY:

Place some of the erasers in a bowl and see if your child can sort them by color, by size or by picture. Give him a piece of card stock paper and some large paper clips, and show her how to clip them onto the paper.

SNACK:

Make a sandwich and place it in a plastic sealable sandwich bag. Place in a lunch bag or lunch box. Add a small box of raisins, an apple cut into slices, a juice box and a wrapped dessert. Your child will enjoy unpacking his lunch and eating it.

OCTOBER: THANKSGIVING

Not what we say about our blessings,
But how we use them,
Is the true measure of our
Thanksgiving

- W. T. Purkiser

BOOKS TO READ:
The Berenstain Bears and the Prize Pumpkin by Stan Berenstain
Thank You Thanksgiving by David Milgrim
Thanksgiving Is Here! by Diane Goode
Thanks for Thanksgiving by Julie Markes

SENSORY BIN:
Place items in the bin for a big Thanksgiving feast. Put a large towel over an overturned box to create a child's table. Fill the bin with all sorts of play food, especially a plastic turkey, corn on the cob, napkins, napkin holders, plates, cutlery, place mats, and bowls. Add any Thanksgiving decorations such as

plastic turkeys and cornucopias. Place in bowls a variety of fillers such as rice, pasta and split peas that she can mix together or put on plates and bowls.

SUPPLEMENTARY ACTIVITY:
Teach your toddler how to use a turkey baster. Place in a larger container two small bowls, one filled with water. Show your child how to use a turkey baster to transfer water to the empty bowl.

Take your toddler for a walk and point out things that you are grateful for: trees, leaves, bus drivers, fire fighters, rocks, etc. Your toddler could bring home some of the things he is grateful for such as twigs, pebbles, and leaves. Then he could make a Thanksgiving Collage.

Check out these videos on YouTube.com:

Bear in the Big Blue House: The Best

Thanksgiving Ever:
http://www.youtube.com/watch?v=KUwC4MMGf7A

Thank You God:
http://www.youtube.com/watch?v=6e30wY5xF6s

SNACK:

Make a Turkey Wrap. Lay on one side of a tortilla the following: 2 slices of roast turkey, slices of avocado, lettuce, sliced tomatoes and mayonnaise. Roll tightly and then slice in quarters.

OCTOBER: HALLOWEEN

Nothing on earth so beautiful as the final haul on Halloween night.

- Steve Almond

BOOKS TO READ:
Halloween Is by Gail Gibbons
And Then Comes Halloween by Tom Brenner
Corduroy's Best Halloween Ever by Don Freeman
Halloween Surprise by Corinne Demas
Jack and Jill: A Halloween Nursery Rhyme by Salina Yoon

SENSORY BIN:
Choose items for Halloween that aren't too scary for a toddler. Pour into your container some dried black beans and white beans. Place in the bin pumpkins, bats, spiders, cats, and a trick or treat basket. Add orange, black and brown pompoms and any other

appropriate items.

SUPPLEMENTARY ACTIVITY:
Buy a large pumpkin and spray shaving cream all over it. Give your child a plastic safety razor with its blade removed and tell him the pumpkin needs a shave. Then wipe the pumpkin down, and use any Mr. and Mrs. Potato Head pieces to make a face on the pumpkin.

SNACK:
Make bagel pumpkins. Cut a bagel in half and smear each side with peanut butter. Give your child small candies and raisins to make faces on their pumpkins.

NOVEMBER: THANKSGIVING (USA)

Thanksgiving Day comes by statute, once a year; to the honest man, it comes as frequently as the heart of gratitude will allow.

- Edward Sandford Martin

BOOKS TO READ:
Thanksgiving at the Tappletons' by Eileen Spinelli
Thanks for Thanksgiving by Heather Patterson
Albert's Thanksgiving by Leslie Tryon
Thanksgiving Treat by Catherine Stock
The Berenstain Bears Give Thanks by Jan Berenstain

SENSORY BIN:
Place items in the bin for a big Thanksgiving feast. Use a cardboard box with a cloth over it for a child's table. Then fill the bin with all sorts of play food, especially a plastic turkey,

corn on the cob, napkins, napkin holders, plates, cutlery, place mats, and bowls. Add any Thanksgiving decorations such as plastic turkeys and cornucopias. Place in bowls a variety of fillers such as rice, pasta and split peas that she can mix together or put on plates and bowls.

SUPPLEMENTARY ACTIVITY:
Check the Supplementary Activities for Canada's Thanksgiving.

Make a Mayflower boat craft with a Styrofoam plate. Add a gob of play dough on the boat and then insert a craft stick into the play dough. Cut from flannel a triangular sail, then cut two small holes in the sail to attach through the craft stick. Place your boat in a bowl of water and pretend you are sailing to the United States.

Make a pilgrim's hat for your toddler to enjoy wearing during this activity: http://www.firstpalette.com/Craft_themes/

Wearables/easypaperhat/easypaperhat.html

Check out these videos on YouTube.com:

Thank You God:
http://www.youtube.com/watch?v=6e30wY5xF6s

Bear In The Big Blue House - The Best Thanksgiving Ever:
http://www.youtube.com/watch?v=KUwC4MMGf7A

SNACK:
Make a Turkey Wrap: Lay on one side of a tortilla the following: 2 slices of roast turkey, slices of avocado, lettuce, sliced tomatoes and mayonnaise. Roll tightly and then slice in quarters.

NOVEMBER: REMEMBRANCE DAY/VETERAN'S DAY

In Flanders Fields the poppies blow
Between the crosses, row on row,
That mark our place, and in the sky
The larks still bravely singing, fly
Scarce heard amid the guns below.

- John McCrae

BOOKS TO READ:
A Poppy Is To Remember by Heather Patterson
Alpha Bravo Charlie: The Military Alphabet by Chris L Demarest
Remembrance Day by Molly Aloian

SENSORY BIN:
Create a hill by pouring a bag of birdseed over two floral craft foams in your container. Give your child some small artificial poppies or other flowers that can be inserted into the floral craft foams. You could also add plastic

vases. Explain that she is planting these flowers as our way of remembering the special people who took care of our country. Also, give her several small flags to insert in one of the floral craft foams. Add into the bin a variety of toy figurines for people that "took care of our country." Then add boats, airplanes, horses, dogs, and land vehicles explaining that the soldiers used these to fight against the bad people.

SUPPLEMENTARY ACTIVITY:
Explain that our country has special songs that are played as we remember these men and women.

Oh Canada Anthem:
http://www.youtube.com/watch?v=ZOY0-MBOh_o

Star Spangled Banner: US National Anthem by the Academy Choirs:
http://www.youtube.com/watch?v=9ETrr-XHBjE

The Last Post:
http://www.youtube.com/watch?v=McCDWYgVyps

SNACK:
Give your child a cupcake and place a national flag on it.

DECEMBER: DECORATING FOR CHRISTMAS

Freshly cut Christmas trees smelling of stars and snow and pine resin - inhale deeply and fill your soul with wintry night . . .

- John Geddes

BOOKS TO READ:
Christmas Tree by Wendell Minor
Turtle and Snake and the Christmas Tree by Kate Spohn
Mr. Willowby's Christmas Tree by Robert Barry
The Berenstain Bears' Christmas Tree by Stan and Jan Berenstain

SENSORY BIN:
Go through your Christmas decorations and choose safe decorations for your child to examine. Fill your container with artificial poinsettia flowers, garland, red and green wooden beads, red and green pompoms,

pinecones, small Christmas stockings, snow globes, jingle bells, Christmas bows, ribbons and small Christmas gift bags. You may also have something that can be wound and plays a Christmas song. You may even be able to find a small tree at Dollar Store and buy a few small ornaments that your toddler can use to decorate the tree. Include any other non-breakable Christmas baking dishes, muffin tins and spoons.

SUPPLEMENTARY ACTIVITY:
Cut out a Christmas spruce tree on a piece of green flannel. If you need a template to do this, check out the following website: http://freebies.about.com/od/Christmas-Freebies/tp/christmas-tree-templates.htm

Give your toddler some colorful buttons, pompoms and glitter glue to decorate this tree. Punch a hole at the top of the tree and tie a ribbon through it so that he can hang it on a Christmas tree.

Paint a pinecone with paint and then sprinkle with glitter.

SNACK:
Make a Vegetable Christmas Tree by making the shape of a tree with either snap peas or pieces of celery. Take a star cookie cutter and cut out a piece of cheese to put on top of the tree. Chop small round pieces of carrots and add dried cranberries and place by the "celery or snap peas" branches.

Finish this Christmas Tree Lunch or snack by serving cookies cut in the shape of a Christmas tree.

DECEMBER: NATIVITY

So the shepherds hurried off and found Mary and Joseph, and the baby, who was lying in the manger. When they had seen him, they spread the word concerning what had been told them about this child.

- Luke 2:16 - 17, Bible

BOOKS TO READ:
Mortimer's Christmas Manger by Karma Wilson
Who Built The Stable? by Ashley Bryan
The Donkey's Christmas Song by Nancy Tafuri
A Christmas Goodnight by Nola Buck

SENSORY BIN:
Add some straw and spread some in one half of a long shallow plastic container. On the other side of the container, add a mixture of beans and lentils. Also add small rocks in the container and any fencing and farm animals that you have from various toy sets. Then add

any small unbreakable nativity items. If you don't have a small stable, just add some building blocks in the container to build one. Attach a small star to a craft stick and place near the manger. Add any greenery such as small trees that are often found with Christmas tree villages.

SUPPLEMENTARY ACTIVITY:
Use red and green play dough. Add some cinnamon to the red play dough and some peppermint extract to the green play dough. Give your child a muffin tin and small cake tin to make a birthday cake and cupcakes for Jesus' birthday out of the play dough. He can decorate the cake with sprinkles, sequins, buttons, and candles.

SNACK:
Give your child a cupcake to decorate with icing and sprinkles. Give him some candles to insert into the cupcake. After you light the candles, the two of you can sing "Happy

Birthday" to Jesus.

CHAPTER 5:

ALPHABETICAL OR TOPICAL SENSORY BINS

The sentence, 'The quick brown fox jumps over a lazy dog' uses every letter in the alphabet.

BEFORE YOU START THESE BINS:

The following bins can be used as topical bins or as one more activity to introduce your child to the letters of the alphabet.

Your goal when you introduce the alphabet is the same goal you have when you introduce any developmental skill to your child. You are giving him as many opportunities as possible to interact with his world and develop his language skills.

Remember that each child's developmental growth varies and is not a reflection of how intelligent she is or how well you are teaching her. You know your child best and you do not want to take the fun out of learning by deciding what she must learn when she isn't ready.

FURTHER ENRICHMENT FOR THE ALPHABET:

1. Help your toddler find the letter you are introducing in the books you are reading to him.
2. Use a variety of letters of the alphabet in various forms such as in craft foam, magnets and letter tiles.
3. Different web-sites have printable alphabet books for each letter that your child can color. Check out the following: http://www.kidzone.ws/kindergarten/learning-letters/books.htm and

http://www.kidsparkz.com

4. Give your toddler a large printed letter. Spread glue on the letter and then give your child some shakers of sand, coarse salt or rice to sprinkle onto the letter. When it dries, show your toddler how to trace the letter with her fingers.

5. Pour sand or coarse salt into a shallow container. Show your child how to trace the letter in the sand.

6. Collect in a basket a variety of toys and household items that start with the letter you are introducing.

7. Give your child a sheet that has dots inside the letter for him to fill in with Do-A-Dot markers or Bingo Daubers. There are some great web-sites that have free printables. Check out the following: http://totschool.shannons.org/do-a-dot-letters/

8. Write on a piece of paper some of the letters you have introduced. Give her a red crayon to mark all the "a's", a blue crayon to mark all the "b's", and so on.

9. Label furniture and toys to increase his

awareness of the letters of the alphabet.
10. Put on the wall a full alphabet so that you can point out various letters to him in your conversation. Begin telling her how Mommy starts with the letter M and how Daddy starts with the letter D.
11. Draw on a sheet of paper the letter and cover it with contact paper or laminate the sheet. Then give your toddler some play dough. Show him how to roll the dough thin and place it on top of the letter.
12. Read to your child a selection of books that introduce all the letters of the alphabet. There are so many alphabet books available that you can often choose a book based on your child's interests. Here are a selection of good alphabet books:

Flower Alphabet Book by Jerry Pallotta
Eating The Alphabet: Fruits and Vegetables from A to Z by Lois Ehlert
Spice Alphabet Book by Jerry Pallotta
The Victory Garden Vegetable Alphabet Book by Jerry Pallotta

The Construction Alphabet Book by Jerry Pallota

The Bird Alphabet Book by Jerry Pallotta

The Icky Bug Alphabet Book by Jerry Pallotta

The Ocean Alphabet Book by Jerry Pallotta

Peanut Butter and Jellyfishes: A Very Silly Alphabet Book by Brian Cleary

M Is For Maple: A Canadian Alphabet by Michael Ulmer

Where Are You Bear? A Canadian Alphabet Adventure by Frieda Wishinsky

Z Is For Zookeeper: A Zoo Alphabet by Marie Smith

Curious George Learns The Alphabet by H.A. Rey

Quilt Alphabet by Lesa Cline-Ransome

Into the A B Sea: An Ocean Alphabet by Deborah Lee Rose

Bang! Boom! Roar! A Busy Crew of Dinosaurs by Nate Evans & Stephanie Gwyn Brown

Shiver Me Letters: A Pirate ABC by June Sobel

Zoo Flakes ABC by Will Howell
B is for Bulldozer: A Construction ABC by June Sobel
Patty's Pumpkin Patch by Teri Sloat
Michael Rosen's ABC by Michael Rosen
The Sleepy Little Alphabet by Judy Sierra

FURTHER ENRICHMENT FOR EACH TOPIC:

1. Give your child a binder that has sheets of card stock paper and sheet protectors to begin her own book called My World Book. Keep in this book a record of all the sensory bins you are introducing to her. Add pages she has colored, photos of her activities, and craft work that can be slipped into a sheet protector. Always ask her what you should write about when you add her work. For example, ask her such questions as what happened in the story you read about the birds? What did you eat for your snack? Did you enjoy it? What do you

want to say about your sensory bin? Each month, you will observe her growing vocabulary and growing ability to tell you more what to write in her book.

2. When you plan each sensory bin, see if there is a place you could take your toddler for his added enjoyment of the topic. For example, when you do the Birds Sensory Bin, take him to a pet store and look at birds.

3. Consider what special clothing your child could wear for each topic to add to her enjoyment.

4. Decide what two or three facts you will share with your toddler about the specific topic. For example, when you study birds, point out that birds can fly because they have wings, explain how birds eat worms, and show from a video how birds hatch from eggs.

LETTER A: ANTS

If ants are such busy workers, how come they find time to go to all the picnics?

- Marie Dressler

BOOKS TO READ:
Ant and Bee by Angela Banner
Ant and Grasshopper by Luli Gray
I Saw an Ant on the Railroad Track by Joshua Prince
I Saw An Ant In A Parking Lot by Joshua Prince
An Ant's Day Off by Bonny Becker
Hey, Little Ant by Phillip and Hannah Hoose

SENSORY BIN:
Place in a container some black beans or dried coffee grounds. Add plastic ants, leaves and flowers. Include some large seeds and explain that ants like to eat seeds. Your toddler will enjoy looking for all the ants either with his shovel or some large tweezers. Make sure you

give him some containers to collect ants. If you have special containers for collecting ants, use them. Share with him how ants live in large families called colonies.

If you have difficulty finding plastic ants, use large black watermelon seeds.

SUPPLEMENTARY ACTIVITY:
Pour some sand into an empty Parmesan container or any other container with holes. Then help your toddler spread glue all over a sheet of construction paper. He may enjoy spreading the glue as finger paint or by using a paintbrush. Have your toddler sprinkle sand onto the paper. Either use some of the plastic ants or large black seeds such as watermelon seeds to glue onto the paper.

SNACK:
Give your toddler some pieces of celery. Put a large dab of peanut butter on the celery for your toddler to spread with his finger or with

a plastic knife. Then give him some raisins for ants to place on the "log."

An alternative snack is to make some dark chocolate pudding and add some raisins.

LETTER B: BIRDS

One must ask children and birds how cherries and strawberries taste.

- Johann Wolfgang Von Goethe

BOOKS TO READ:
Are You My Mother? by P. D. Eastman
Lowly Worm Meets the Early Bird by Richard Scarry
Baby Bird by Joyce Dunbar
The Best Nest by P. D. Eastman
My "b" Sound Box by Jane Moncure

SENSORY BIN:
Pour into your plastic container a bag of birdseed. Then add any plastic birds that you have found at the Dollar Store or that your child has in other toy sets. Also, add any bird houses, twigs, small rocks, plastic eggs, long strands of cooked spaghetti for worms, and feathers.

After some of your child's discoveries, make sure you bring to his attention how birds have wings and we do not. Why do birds have feathers? What do birds live in? If a bird is sitting on an egg in her nest, what is going to happen?

SUPPLEMENTARY ACTIVITY:
Give your child some play dough, twigs, pebbles, feathers, strands of wool, and pieces of pipe cleaners to make a bird's nest. Then give him several wrapped chocolate eggs or jelly beans to place on the nest.

Give your child a feather to dip into some paint and use as a brush on a sheet of paper. When the paint is dry, glue some feathers on the page.

Check out these videos on YouTube.com:

Baby Robin Hatching:
http://www.youtube.com/watch?v=FDKgLfWheoI

Robin Bird Nest Eggs Hatched and Baby Starlings On Front Porch Father Visits and Feeds:
http://www.youtube.com/watch?v=7yqCIceJj_c

SNACK:

Make some Rice Krispies Squares into nests. Then add some jelly beans or chocolate eggs into the nests.

LETTER C: CAMPING

The fire is the main comfort of the camp, whether in summer or winter, and is about as ample at one season as at another. It is as well for cheerfulness as for warmth and dryness.

- Henry David Thoreau

BOOKS TO READ:
Olivia Goes Camping by Alex Harvey
When We Go Camping by Margriet Ruurs & Andrew Kiss
Fred and Ted Go Camping by Peter Eastman
Maisy Goes Camping by Lucy Cousins
Curious George Goes Camping by Margaret Rey & H.A. Rey
Just Me and My Dad by Mercer Mayer
My "c" Sound Box by Jane Moncure

SENSORY BIN:
Add sand, sea shells, a group of twigs for logs, plastic trees, rocks, and pine cones. You could also add some small figurines as campers.

Take some firm card stock paper and cut in half. Then fold one of the sheets of paper in half to make a tent. Place a small foil dish in the bin and add some twigs in it .Then scrunch small pieces of tissue paper and add to the foil dish to make the pretend fire. Besides having a campsite bin, you could have an additional bin for boating and swimming near the campsite! Simply add some blue food coloring to the water and add boats and plastic fish.

SUPPLEMENTARY ACTIVITY:
Create a campsite for your child to do some role playing. Set up a small tent or make a tent by placing a blanket over a table. Inside the tent, place a rolled towel tied with a string for a bedroll. Beside the bedroll, leave a child's binoculars, flashlight, and lantern. The binoculars can be easily made by gluing together two empty toilet cardboard tubes. Then punch a hole on each side and attach some string to make a strap.

Outside the tent, you could set up a lawn chair and small picnic table or an overturned cardboard box. Include a container of play food, plates and cups.

SNACK:
Make a popular camping treat called S'mores. Place a graham wafer on a plate. Top with chocolate chips or a piece of chocolate bar and then add a marshmallow. Microwave until marshmallow puffs - about 15 seconds. Remove from the microwave and cover with another graham wafer. Make sure it isn't too hot when you serve it to your toddler.

LETTER D: DINOSAURS

I believe implicitly that every young man in the world is fascinated with either sharks or dinosaurs.

- Peter Benchley

BOOKS TO READ:
Curious George: Dinosaur Tracks by Julie Tibbott
Oh My Oh My Oh Dinosaurs! by Sandra Boynton
The Berenstain Bears' Dinosaur Dig by Jan Berenstain
Curious George's Dinosaur Discovery by H.A. Rey
Dinosaur Roar! by Paul Stickland
Bones, Bones, Dinosaur Bones by Byron Barton
My "d" Sound Box by Jane Moncure

SENSORY BIN:
Place in a long shallow container some small boxes and plastic containers turned upside

down to create some hills for the dinosaurs. Then pour some bird seed or green colored rice into the container and over your "hills." (Recipe on Page 16) Add any of the following: greenery such as plastic palm trees, small rocks, plastic dinosaurs, plastic eggs, and some plastic eggs filled with plastic dinosaurs.

Bury some of the dinosaurs, and stand others on the "hills." If you have a drying rack or cookie rack, place it on top of a second container so that when your toddler uses her small shovel to find the buried dinosaurs, she will have fun pouring the bird seed on top of this "sifter" and discovering buried dinosaurs. After discovering her buried dinosaurs, show her how to use a paint brush to brush off the "dirt" to clean them.

SUPPLEMENTARY ACTIVITY:
You will need some play dough and your child's plastic dinosaurs that you used in her sensory bin. For added texture, add sand or bird sand to the play dough. Show your child

how to build an "egg" around her small dinosaurs with play dough. Then she will enjoy "finding" them again. Also, show him how to make footprints in some flattened play dough with his dinosaurs.

SNACK:

Place small candies or cookies that are in the shape of dinosaurs in a fruit dish. Crush some Oreos or graham wafers and add to the fruit dish. Pour some apple sauce or chocolate pudding on top of the mixture.

LETTER E: EGGS

I do not like green eggs and ham, I do not like them Sam I am.

- Dr. Seuss, Green Eggs & Ham

BOOKS TO READ:
First the Egg by Laura Vaccaro Seeger
Egg by Alex T. Smith
Green Eggs and Ham by Dr. Seuss
Minerva Louise and the Colorful Eggs by Janet M. Stoeke
My "e" Sound Box by Jane Moncure

SENSORY BIN:
Collect at least a dozen egg shells, then boil them in water to sterilize them. Place a selection of shells in several jars that have been filled with water, and each filled with a different color of food coloring. When the eggs are colored, dry the shells on a cookie sheet. When they are dried, place these shells into your sensory bin.

Give your toddler a child's hammer, a pail and a scoop. Add some plastic eggs for him to fill and pour. The eggshells may be a little sharp so you may want to put some mittens on his hands.

SUPPLEMENTARY ACTIVITY:
Your toddler will be making an egg shell mosaic. Spread glue all over a sheet of construction paper or a paper plate. Then give your toddler a bowl of the colored egg shells to pour onto the paper or paper plate. When the glue dries, shake off the excess egg shells.

Check out this video on YouTube.com:

The Bird and the Egg:
http://www.youtube.com/user/HooplaKidzTv?v=q788sm902LY

SNACK:
Make some egg salad sandwiches with your child's help.

LETTER F: FARM

Life on a farm is a school of patience; you can't hurry the crops or make an ox in two days.

- Henri Alain

BOOKS TO READ:
A Visit to The Farm by B. A. Hoena
My Farm Friends by Wendell Minor
The Berenstain Bears Down On The Farm by Stan Berenstain
The Noisy Farm: Lots of Animal Noises to Enjoy by Marni McGee
My "f" Sound Box by Jane Moncure

SENSORY BIN:
Set out three shallow plastic or foil containers and fill one with popcorn, the second one with bird seed and the third one with straw.

Set in a container all your farm items such as tractors, animals and fencing. Your child will enjoy deciding where she wants to set up the animals. Include smaller bowls of oatmeal, sugar cubes and grass (from Easter) that your child can use as food for the animals. Of course, include scoops that she will enjoy using with the three different kinds of filler.

SUPPLEMENTARY ACTIVITY:
Print from the following website pictures of farm animals and their young. Then place the mother animals on the table and give her one card at a time of the accompanying baby animal to match with its mother.
http://www.sparklebox.co.uk/previews/7651-7675/sb7667-farm-animals-and-their-young-matching-cards.html#.UW24M7-fv9E

SNACK:
Make an 'Egg in a Hole' by cutting a hole in a slice of bread. Grease your skillet and when it is hot, lay the slice of bread in it. Toast about 2 minutes and then flip over. Crack an egg into the hole and season with salt and pepper. Cook according to how you like your eggs.

LETTER G: GARDEN

If you have a garden and a library, you have everything you need.

- Marcus T. Cicero

BOOKS TO READ:
A Green, Green Garden by Mercer Mayer
Grandma's Garden by Mercer Mayer
Surprise Garden (Molly and Emmett) by Marylin Hafner
Paddington Bear In The Garden by Michael Bond
My "g" Sound Box by Jane Moncure

SENSORY BIN:
Fill your container with dirt or a combination of different lentils. Once you have filled a container with your filler, fill another container with items for her to plant: small toy vegetables, small plastic plants, plastic flowers and dried beans. Place them in a bucket for him to plant. Your child will need

some children's gardening tools to use for planting and digging.

Place in a bowl some plastic worms or strands of cooked spaghetti. Encourage your child to bury the worms in the dirt as you explain how the worms help the plants to grow. Include any small pots for planting vegetables.

If you are outside for this bin, give him a small watering can and spray bottle filled with water. Indoors, you will most likely want him to have pretend water!

SUPPLEMENTARY ACTIVITY:
Fill a clear plastic cup with dirt, sprinkle some grass seeds on top and cover with more soil. Water until moist. Explain to your child that the grass seeds will grow as long as they get enough water and sun. It will probably take 7 or 8 days before your child will begin to see some tiny sprouts and then each week, he will see the grass growing longer.

For extra fun, create a face on the cup by gluing googly eyes and pieces of construction paper for its nose, mouth and ears. When the grass gets quite long, you could even help him use scissors to give the grass a haircut.

SNACK:
Place a selection of fruits and vegetables on a plate and explain how these all came from a garden.

LETTER H: HATS

That's the thing about hats. They're extravagant and full of humour and allow for a sense of costume, but in a lighthearted way.

- Stephen Jones

BOOKS TO READ:
Hat by Paul Hoppe
The Hat by Jan Brett
Which Hat Is That? by Anna G. Hines
Magritte's Marvelous Hat by D. B. Johnson
Hats Hats Hats by Blaine Klippenstein
My "h" Sound Box by Jane Moncure

SENSORY BIN:
This bin is not typical since your child has nothing to pour into other containers. However, he is having lots of sensory fun touching hats and experiencing how they feel on his head. Add all sorts of hats that your child can enjoy wearing: party hat, hockey helmet, baseball cap, sun hat, winter hat, rain

hat, hard hat, firefighter's hat, policeman's hat, chef's hat, cowboy hat, baby hat. After she has tried them on, have her sort them by size or color.

Be sure to include a mirror so that your toddler can see her new look in the mirror.

SUPPLEMENTARY ACTIVITY:
Play some music and whenever you stop the music, she changes her hat.

Make a hat. Glue or tape bows and ribbons on a paper plate or a foam visor. If you use a paper plate, punch a hole on each side and add long ribbons or elastic ribbon to tie under your child's chin.

Place a large hat on the floor and give your child a small ball to throw into it.

SNACK:
Take a hat of your toddler's choice, line its

inside with foil and add some treats.

LETTER I: INSECTS

If all insects on earth disappeared, within 50 years, all life on Earth would end. If all human beings disappeared from the Earth, within 50 years, all forms of life would flourish.

- Jonas Salk

BOOKS TO READ:
Ant! Ant! Ant! by April P Sayre
I Love Bugs! by Emma Dodd
I Love Bugs by Philemon Sturges
Bugs! Bugs! Bugs! by Bob Barner
Creepy Crawly Calypso by Richard Love
My "I" Sound Box by Jane Moncure

SENSORY BIN:
Use dirt or green split peas as your filler. Add silk leaves, sticks, rocks, pine cones and plastic insects to your container. Give your child an insect container, magnifying glass, a bucket and shovel for his explorations.

SUPPLEMENTARY ACTIVITY:
Go for a walk looking for insects under rocks, in bushes, and in gardens.

Print a matching game called "Buggy Friends Shadow Match" from the following website: http://www.busylittlebugs.com.au/freebie-friday-buggy-friends-shadow-match/

Print an Insects Memory Game from the following website: http://busybeekidsprintables.s3.amazonaws.com/animals/insects/games/InsectMemoryGame.pdf

SNACK:
Make some ants sitting on a log: Give your child a piece of celery and show him how to spread some peanut butter or cream cheese on it. Add some raisins.

Make a ladybug: Cut a cored apple in half and lay it side down on a plate. Place some peanut butter in a small fruit dish. Let your child put his finger into the peanut butter and then spread it on the apple. Then give him some raisins to put on top of the peanut butter. Stick two toothpicks at the end of the apple and add raisins on each of the toothpicks for antennae.

Make a caterpillar: Cut 4 slices of banana. Stick the slices together by placing peanut butter between the slices. Place two pretzel sticks in a V-shape at the front of the bananas. Insert a grape on to the two pretzels.

LETTER J: JUNGLE

On a hard jungle journey, nothing is so important as having a team you can trust.

- Tahir Shah

BOOKS TO READ:
Way Far Away On a Wild Safari by Jan Peck
Starry Safari by Linda Ashman
We Get Giggly On a Safari! by Linda Kaszap
Walking Through The Jungle by Fred Penner

SENSORY BIN:
Glue some moss all around a floral craft foam and glue some blue flannel on a flat Styrofoam tray or paper plate. Fill your bin with green colored rice and then add the floral craft foam that can be a cliff or hill and the flannel for pretend water.

Place some animals in a container for your child to enjoy setting up in the bin. You could also add any plastic fencing your child may have from any of his toys. Provide your child some greenery that your toddler could plant" in her floral craft foam.

SUPPLEMENTARY ACTIVITY:
Have fun with this jungle theme by giving your child some dress up clothes to go on a safari such as a wide brim hat. You could even take a large paper bag apart, cut it in half, then cut open some arm holes to make a vest.

Take the jungle animals and place them throughout the house. Make a trail of scented cotton balls to the animals using various scented oils: peppermint extract, vanilla extract, almond extract, or any essential oils that you may have. Tell your child that she is going to use her sense of smell to find the animals just as animals find each other through their sense of smell.

SNACK:
Cut a banana in half and insert a craft stick

into each half; Roll each banana half in chocolate syrup. Then roll it in some coconut. Freeze and then serve.

Make a Jungle Smoothie by blending an orange, a banana, a pineapple and some coconut water.

LETTER K: KITES

Kites rise highest against the wind, not with it.

- Winston Churchill

BOOKS TO READ:
The Kite by Luis Garay
Kite Day: A Bear and Mole Story by Will Hillenbrand
The Most Beautiful Kite in the World by Andrea Spalding
Curious George Flies A Kite by Margret Rey

SENSORY BIN:
This sensory bin explores how wind makes a kite and other things move. It will help your toddler better appreciate the use of the wind when you go outside to fly a kite with your toddler.

You will need a fan and a hair dryer that is set on cool, to blow air on various items. Your child will enjoy catching the item as it floats down. Vary the speed of air for your child to see what happens. In your sensory bin, include tissue paper, streamers, taped streamers around a paper bowl, a small flag, and a leaf.

This activity requires your constant supervision and help as he will need your assistance to blow things in front of the fan. Talk about how a kite needs this wind to keep it flying high into the sky.

SUPPLEMENTARY ACTIVITY:
Attach some long streamers and ribbons to a balloon and attach one end of a long string to the balloon and the other end to your child's wrist. Go outside and fly his "kite".

Give your child a feather, a ping pong ball and a cotton ball to blow across a table. See if you and your toddler can keep a feather up in the air as you both blow on it. Explain to your child that the air you are both blowing is much like the wind outside.

Check out this video on YouTube.com:

How To Fly A Kite:
http://www.youtube.com/watch?v=5X8wwHpqeU0

SNACK:
Cut bread into diamond shapes. Then give your child some peanut butter or jam or both to spread on the bread. Add some thin red licorice as its tail.

Make some Jello Jigglers and give your child a kite-shaped or diamond shaped cookie cutter. http://www.kraftrecipes.com/recipes/jell-oo-jiggler-53920.aspx

LETTER L: LADYBUGS

With a butterfly kiss and a ladybug hug, sleep tight little one like a bug in a rug.

- Author Unknown.

BOOKS TO READ:
Ladybugs by Monica Hughes
Ladybugs by Barrie Watts
Crawl, Ladybug, Crawl! by Dana Meachen Rau
The Grouchy Ladybug by Eric Carle
The Very Lazy Ladybug by Isobel Finn

SENSORY BINS:
Add some green colored rice to your container. (Recipe on Page 16) Place some leaves and twigs around the container and add the ladybugs. Party stores often have plastic ladybugs and other ladybug paraphernalia since this is a popular children's birthday theme party. Also, add some roses and explain that roses often have aphids that ladybugs like

to eat.

A great addition to your sensory bin is red plastic bowls. Show your toddler how to add black sticker dots to the red bowls.

SUPPLEMENTARY ACTIVITY:
Go outside and look around shrubs and rose bushes for ladybugs.
Make some Rock Ladybugs. Paint the rock red and let dry. Then give your child some black dot stickers and googly eyes to place on her ladybug.

Check out these videos on YouTube.com:

Karyn Henley - Five Little Ladybugs:
http://www.youtube.com/watch?v=Ep0cPZDtwD8

Frank Leto's Ladybug Ladybug Song:
http://www.youtube.com/watch?v=qjhSgMqsAfM

SNACK:

Cut an apple into two halves. Create spots with almond butter or peanut butter on the red skin of the apple. Add raisins or chocolate chips or cranberries on top of the peanut butter for the lady bug spots. Add two toothpicks with raisins on their ends for antennae.

LETTER M: MAIL

I've always felt there is something sacred in a piece of paper that travels the earth from hand to hand, head to head, heart to heart.

- Robert Michael Pyle

BOOKS TO READ:
Bunny Mail by Rosemary Wells
The Giant Hug by Sandra Horning
Caillou Sends a Letter by Joceline Sanschagrin
Send It! by Don Carter
Penguin Post by Debi Gliori

SENSORY BIN:
Fill a container with the following: postcards, junk mail, boxes to sort mail, packages, magazines, stamps, return address labels, scotch tape to wrap parcels, a mailbox (see Supplementary Activity), envelopes, and birthday cards. Add some small toys wrapped in a large brown envelope or box. Give him several small boxes and pretend they are

either parcels or mail boxes where he can deliver mail.

SUPPLEMENTARY ACTIVITY:
Make a mail box by taking a shoe box, cut a slot into it and wrap it in wrapping paper. Cut a rectangular piece of construction paper to make a flag. Attach the flag to the box with a brass paper fastener. When you have added mail to the box for your toddler, place the flag up. Set up this mailbox in her room so that you can deliver mail to her on a regular basis. It doesn't have to be complicated; you can give her junk mail that you have received, any used cards or post cards, a coloring page, a small Dollar Store toy, etc.
Take some of the items in the sensory bin and help your toddler sort them according to size.

Check out these videos on YouTube.com:

Postman Pat Theme Song:
http://www.youtube.com/watch?v=HiFNt8nGffA

Postman Pat: Runaway Train:
http://www.youtube.com/watch?v=kXl81VPcjZI

SNACK:
Put a snack such as dried fruit in various sizes of envelopes.

LETTER N: NURSES

The trained nurse has become one of the great blessings of humanity, taking a place beside the physician and the priest.

- William Osler

BOOKS TO READ:
Doctor Ted by Andrea Beaty
Going to the Doctor by Anne Civardi
The Berenstain Bears Go to the Doctor by Stan & Jan Berenstain
Maisy Goes to The Hospital by Lucy Cousins
I Want To Be A Nurse by Dan Liebman
We Need Nurses by Lola Schaefer

SENSORY BIN:
Place a small blanket over a coffee table or child's table to make a hospital bed or a doctor's table in his office. Place the following medical items in a variety of containers for him to play with and to take care of the medical needs of his dolls and plush animals:

a face cloth, band aids, gauze, glasses with no lenses, tissues, a large cosmetic bag for medical kit, empty pill containers, small blankets or towels, cotton balls, nail file, Q-Tips, eye dropper, and craft sticks.

If your child has a medical kit, add all of those items as well. It will most likely have a stethoscope, a needle and thermometer.

Cut some felt into strips long enough to wrap around your child's dolls and plush animals for a tensor bandage. Add some velcro on each strip.

SUPPLEMENTARY ACTIVITY:
Give your child a selection of band aids, gauze, and cotton balls to make a collage on a sheet of construction paper.

Have your toddler stand on your weight scale and record his weight. Have him stand against a wall and record his height.

Give your toddler several Mr. Potato Heads and some play dough. Tell him Mr. and Mrs. Potato Heads have broken arms and need you to make casts for them.

Make your child a Nurse's Cap to wear. Check out the following web-site for template and instructions:
http://www.daniellesplace.com/html/doctor-nurse-crafts.html

Check out this video on YouTube.com:

Animated Music Video: Nurses Making a Difference:
http://www.youtube.com/watch?v=fpSzlFjPoU0

SNACK:
Serve your toddler Chicken Noodle Soup and tell her that when people have a cold, they often feel better eating this soup.

LETTER O: OCEANS

There is nothing more beautiful than the way the ocean refuses to stop kissing the shoreline, no matter how many times it is sent away.

- Sarah Kay

BOOKS TO READ:
Wow! Ocean! by Robert Neubecker
The Ocean Is by Kathy Kranking
I'm the Best Artist In The Ocean by Kevin Sherry
Hello Ocean by Pam M. Ryan
Wave by Suzy Lee

SENSORY BIN:
Before you introduce this ocean bin to your child, show her on a world globe or map the ocean.

Fill your container with water, and then add some blue food coloring. Set in various containers: sea creatures, colored gems, rocks, pebbles, aquarium rock, leaves, and boats. Let your child enjoy adding these items into her ocean. If you are doing this activity indoors, you can always turn your bath tub into an ocean to keep the water contained! However, you may want to place some bath towels on the bottom of the tub to prevent any scratches from the rocks and pebbles.

SUPPLEMENTARY ACTIVITY:
Help your child make a wave bottle. You will need a plastic jar, an empty Gatorade bottle or a plastic baby bottle. Give your child a large spoon to add several spoonfuls of aquarium gravel or sand. Now add several small sea shells and plastic sea creatures. Fill the bottle half full of water.

Next, add baby oil until almost full. Your child will enjoy using a funnel as you help her pour the baby oil. Add in a drop of blue food coloring. You could also add some glitter. Put the lid on and secure the lid tightly with masking tape. Lay the bottle on its side and enjoy the ocean.

Rub a damp sponge over a sheet of finger paint paper. Pour some blue finger paint onto the paper. Let your child swirl the paint across the paper to create an ocean picture. Then give your child some sand in a shaker to sprinkle on her page. She could also add fish and whale stickers when the paint is dry.

SNACK:
Make some blue Jello and when it has slightly thickened, add some fish crackers.

LETTER P: PIRATES

Yo Ho! Yo Ho! A Pirate's Life for Me!

- Pirates of the Caribbean

BOOKS TO READ:
Pajama Pirates by Andrew Kramer
Shiver Me Letters: A Pirate ABC by June Sobel
Do Pirates Take Baths? by Kathy Tucker
Captain Flinn and the Pirate Dinosaurs by Giles Andreae
Pirates Don't Take Baths by John Segal
The Night Pirates by Peter Harris

SENSORY BIN:
Fill your bin with black beans and begin hiding "treasure" in your container. Such items as the following work well: beads, necklaces, gem stones, gold coins, real coins, old rings or plastic rings. When these have all been buried, place a small treasure box (a decorated shoe box) on top of the filler. Add

any small pirate items you may have.
Place on top of this bin a child's shovel and pail. Include several items such as a small jewelry bag, a pretty box or a jewelry box that could be used to collect the rings and beads. Provide a piggy bank to collect the real coins.

SUPPLEMENTARY ACTIVITY:
Tie a bandana around your child's head and tell him he is going to do the Pirate Dance. Play some fast uplifting music and twirl together around the room.

Check out the following web-site for a simple Pirate hat to make from construction paper: http://www.leehansen.com/printables/masks/pirate-hat.htm

Download and print a Printable Pirates Memory Game from the following web-site: http://www.kidscraps.com/GameCentral/MemoryGames/memorycards02/MC-pirates.htm

SNACK:
Set a small pirate toy or a gold wrapped chocolate on a piece of cake or cupcake.

LETTER Q: QUILTS

Quilting is my passion. Chocolate comes in a close second.

BOOKS TO READ:
The Kindness Quilt by Nancy Wallace
Papa and the Pioneer Quilt by Jean Van Leeuwen
Oma's Quilt by Paulette Bourgeois
Selina and the Bear Paw Quilt by Barbara Smucker

SENSORY BIN:
Cut construction paper and scrapbook paper into squares, circles and triangles, and place in a container. Add a variety of fabric scraps such as cotton, jersey, flannel and minky. Add cotton balls and small plastic people to your bin. Give your toddler tweezers and tongs to play with these pieces. Make sure you give her several bowls to transfer pieces to and from.

Cut holes in the center of some of the fabric shapes. Add a shoelace to "sew" the pieces together. Attach one piece of fabric to the shoelace and tie a knot so the rest of the pieces added do not slide off.

SUPPLEMENTARY ACTIVITY:
Give your child a sheet of paper, a selection of the pieces of paper from her bin, and some glue. Cover the page with glue and then tell her to make a beautiful paper quilt by covering the page with the various shapes of paper.

Use pieces of paper from the bin to sort by shape and by color.

Do you have a quilt or do you know of someone who has a quilt? What a great sensory experience just to be wrapped up in a quilt and reading books together! You could look closely at all the squares in the quilt and talk about them.

SNACK:

Give your child a slice of bread. Cut some cheese into several different shapes that can fit altogether on a slice of bread. Tell her she is making a bread quilt as she places the cheese on the bread.

LETTER R: ROCKS

What are men to rocks and mountains?

- Jane Austen, Pride and Prejudice

BOOKS TO READ:
If Rocks Could Sing: A Discovered Alphabet by Leslie McGuirk
Everybody Needs a Rock by Byrd Baylor
Let's Go Rock Collecting by Roma Gans
Stones: Eyelike Nature by Play Bac
Billy's Pet Rock by Tim Healey

SENSORY BIN:
Set up a rock collection for your toddler to enjoy shoveling and transferring to other containers. If he has a dump truck, he will enjoy loading the rocks on it. You will also want to give him a pail, shovel, any kinds of scoops, and containers. Include a variety of sizes, shapes and colors of rocks. After he has had fun playing with the rocks, give him a container of water. Your toddler will also

need an assortment of cleaning tools such as a sponge, a spray bottle filled with water, a brush, and a cloth to clean the rocks. Lay out a towel for him to place the washed rocks.

Don't expect great cleaning or that he will methodically clean all the rocks, but he will have fun with this addition of water! This activity can be done indoors, but certainly it is simpler to do it outside.

SUPPLEMENTARY ACTIVITY:
Go for a walk and collect some rocks that you can add to your bin.

Set out three rocks so that he can sort by size: small, medium, large. Then give him more rocks to sort by size.

Decorate some rocks. Pour some paint into a plastic container that has a secure lid. Then let your toddler shake the container. When you open the container, take out the rock and let it dry. If he enjoyed shaking the container, give him more rocks to do. When the rocks are dried, give him some googly eyes and stickers to decorate the rocks.

SNACK:
Show your child how some food he eats has stones in them: peaches, plums, nectarines, avocados, cherries. Enjoy eating a selection of these fruits.

LETTER S: SEEDS

Anyone can count the seeds in an apple, but only God can count the number of apples in a seed.

- Robert Schuller

BOOKS TO READ:
The Tiny Seed by Eric Carle
How Many Seeds In A Pumpkin by Margaret McNamara
Plant A Little Seed by Bonnie Christensen
One Watermelon Seed by Celia Lottridge
One Little Seed by Elaine Greenstein

SENSORY BIN:
You will need some packets of seeds, some small containers for potting, gloves, gardening tools for a child, a watering can, and some plastic flowers and vegetables. Pour into your container some dirt if you are doing this outside or black beans if you are doing it indoors. You can also use dried coffee grounds that are closer to the texture of dirt.

SUPPLEMENTARY ACTIVITY:
Make a fridge magnet. Cut a circle from a piece of firm cardboard. Have your child paint the cardboard. Spread white glue on the circle and glue on various large seeds such as pumpkin seeds. When it is dry, attach magnet strips to the back of the cardboard.

Trace a large S on a sheet of paper and show her how to glue seeds on the S.

Check out these videos on YouTube.com:

Time lapse radish seeds sprouting:
http://www.youtube.com/watch?v=d26AhcKeEbE
After watching the video of the time lapse of radish seeds sprouting, give your toddler some radish seeds to plant in a small pot. Let her water it daily and watch it grow.

How Do Plants Grow?:
http://www.youtube.com/watch?v=xldSRWtNMXE

SNACK:
Give your child a slice of watermelon and have her take out the seeds before she eats it.

LETTER T: TURTLES

Researchers identify turtles by the different patterns on the turtle's shell. It is like a fingerprint - different on every one.

- Patrick Thompson

BOOKS TO READ:
Where Should Turtle Be? by Susan Ring
Turtle Splash! Countdown at the Pond by Cathryn Falwell
Scoot! by Cathryn Falwell
Emma's Turtle by Eve Bunting

SENSORY BIN:
Give your toddler a container of water and in another container, add the following: aquarium rocks, gems, turtles, and fish. Give your child an aquarium net and a scoop to catch the turtles. Set out another container that has leaves and flowers where the turtle can be placed when your toddler takes it out of the water. Explain how some turtles like to

eat leaves, flowers and fish.

SUPPLEMENTARY ACTIVITY:

You will need a paper plate and some torn pieces of brown and green construction paper to make a turtle. Spread glue over the bottom of the plate. Let your child glue all the pieces of construction paper on the plate to make the turtle's back.

Cut a black circle, add two googly eyes, and glue on one end of the plate. Cut four legs and a tail from green construction paper and show your toddler where to glue these pieces. When it is dry, tape the turtle craft on the back of your child and encourage him to crawl on the floor like a turtle.

SNACK:

Use a package of refrigerated biscuit dough to make Turtle Shaped Biscuits. You will need two biscuits for each turtle. Lay on a cookie sheet on of the biscuits for the turtle's body.

Then take the second biscuit, cut off a piece and shape it into a ball for its head and attach to the body. With the rest of the biscuit, make five very small balls for its feet and tail and attach to the body. For extra fun, use a black food decorator pen and give the turtle two eyes.

LETTER U: UMBRELLAS

It's no use carrying an umbrella if your shoes are leaking.

- Irish Proverb

BOOKS TO READ:
Umbrella by Taro Yashima
The Umbrella by Ingrid Schubert
The Umbrella by Jan Brett
One Rainy Day by Christina Butler
One Rainy Day by Valeri Gorbachev

SENSORY BIN:
Do this sensory bin in the bathtub to more easily contain the water. However, if you choose to use a plastic container, place a large plastic table cloth or shower curtain under the bin.

This is a bin very easy to prepare since you just put some water into the bath tub and give your child various supplies to "make rain."

Include colanders, strainers, large eye droppers, and a child's watering can. For added fun, hold an umbrella over your child and tell her that you think it is going to start raining. Include music from YouTube of rain falling to make the experience even more exciting. Then take a wet sponge and begin squeezing the water on top of your child's umbrella.

SUPPLEMENTARY ACTIVITY:
Give your child an umbrella and go for a walk outside. It would be even more enjoyable if you did this on a rainy day or at least after it rains.

Play some music like "Singing In The Rain" and let your toddler walk holding the umbrella open. Stop the music regularly and explain that when it stops, she must lower the umbrella.

Tape some squares of bubble wrap on the floor. Now have your child jump into the bubble wrap puddles.

Give your child a paper towel or a coffee filter and some watered down blue paint. Give her a large eye dropper to transfer the paint to her painting surface.

SNACK:
Have your toddler help you decorate cupcakes by inserting small paper umbrellas in each one.

LETTER V: VETERINARIANS

The best doctor in the world is a veterinarian. He can't ask his patients what is the matter - - he's got to just know.

- Will Rogers

BOOKS TO READ:
Olivia Becomes A Vet by Alex Harvey
Hairy Maclary's Rumpus at the Vet by Lynley Dodd
Sally Goes to the Vet by Stephen Huneck
Doctor Maisy by Lucy Cousins

SENSORY BIN:
Set up a table or overturn a large cardboard box and place a large towel or small table cloth on top of it for your child's work area. Place in your container any items that your child could use when he plays the role of veterinarian. Give him any of the following: animal food dishes, small dog collars, balls, dog toys, brushes, and a container of pet food

which could be split peas. Include old baby blankets, play food such as meats, vegetables and fruits, a brush, band aids, gauze, disposable gloves, craft stick, medical syringe, bottle for pretend medicine, thermometer, cotton balls, cosmetic bag, a baby bottle, and a child's medical kit. For added fun, give your toddler an old white shirt to wear as his veterinarian costume.

Line up all his plush animals in his "waiting room."

SUPPLEMENTARY ACTIVITY:
Go to a pet store and look at the cats, guinea pigs, dogs, hamsters, birds, etc.

Buy a box of small dog treats that contain many colors for the following activities:
- Use them to help your child sort by color.
- Use the biscuits to create patterns. See if he can repeat that pattern. For example, two colors of the same and

then 3 colors of the next form a pattern.
- Give him a thin piece of cardboard, spread with glue and ask her to make a Dog Bone Collage.

SNACK:

Use a dog bone cookie cutter for this snack or cut out the shape of a dog bone with a knife. Take several slices of bread and create dog bone shapes. Add some peanut butter or almond butter. You could also make some Rice Krispies Squares and cut into dog bone shapes.

LETTER W: WORMS

The message is not so much that the worms will inherit the Earth, but that all things play a role in nature, even the lowly worm.

- Gary Larson

BOOKS TO READ:
Bob and Otto by Robert Bruel
Inch by Inch by Leo Lionni
Yucky Worms by Vivian French
Diary of a Worm by Doreen Cronin

SENSORY BIN:
Pour dirt, black beans or black water beads into your bin. Hide various lengths of cooked strands of spaghetti for worms or add plastic worms. Give your child tongs and tweezers to find the worms. Add some small artificial plants to plant in the dirt. Explain that worms help plants to grow.

SUPPLEMENTARY ACTIVITY:

Pour some finger paint on a sheet of finger paint paper. Then give your child some of the cooked spaghetti strands to move across the paint to make worm tracks. Your child could also use the plastic worms from the bin.

Have your child wiggle on her stomach pretending to be a worm.

Go outside if weather permits and begin digging in some soil to look for worms. An alternative is to buy some worms at a fishing store. Place the worm on a paper plate and watch the worm wiggle. Ask her if she wants to touch the worm gently. Talk about whether worms have legs, arms and a mouth, and where they like to live.

SNACK:

Pour some dark chocolate pudding into a dish. Then crush some dark brown cookies into the pudding and add some gummy worms.

LETTER X: BOX

Kids don't like being put into boxes, and your kid can act in different ways in different situations.

- Rosalind Wiseman

BOOKS TO READ:
The Kiss Box by Bonnie Verburg
Fox on a Box by Phil Cox
My Book Box by Will Hillenbrand
Harry's Box by Angela McAllister
The Big Brown Box by Marisabina Russo
My Cat Likes To Hide in Boxes by Eve Sutton
My "x, y, z" Sound Box by Jane Moncure

SENSORY BIN:
There are not many words that begin with X that work well for a sensory bin, so we decided to use a word that ends in X.

You will need a variety of sizes of boxes to place in the bin. In each box, fill it with different types of items. Use items that he hasn't seen in a while to increase his surprise as he takes off the lids. Inside the boxes, you might add any of the following: plastic animals, plastic sea creatures, small cars, wooden beads, buttons, pompoms, rocks, alphabet letters, ribbons and bows, and small balls.

When your toddler has finished opening each box and has enjoyed seeing what is inside, give him various scoops, spoons, ladles and tongs to help him move the items. He could line up the boxes or stack the boxes to make special homes for his items. Also, he can practice finding the correct lid for each box.

SUPPLEMENTARY ACTIVITY:
Give your child a small box - perhaps one of his shoe boxes - to decorate. Place a large X on the lid of the box using masking tape. Give your child some paint and paint the lid. When the paint dries, take off the masking tape. Paint the rest of the box and then add

stickers, glitter glue and small pieces of ribbon to decorate the sides of the box.

SNACK:
Make a box lunch for your child. If the paint has dried on the box he has painted, use that box.

LETTER Y: YARN

It is pure potential. Every ball or skein of yarn holds something inside it, and the great mystery of what that might be can be almost spiritual"

- Stephanie Pearl-McPhee, Knitting Rules!: The Yarn Harlot's Bag of Knitting Tricks

BOOKS TO READ:
Extra Yarn by Mac Barnett
Knitting Nell by Julie J. Roth
Annie Hoot and the Knitting Extravaganza by Holly Clifton-Brown
Charlie Needs a Cloak by Tomie DePaola
Little Lamb, Have You Any Wool? by Isabel M. Martins
My "x, y, z" Book by Jane Moncure

SENSORY BIN:
Put a variety of lengths and colors of yarn in a bin. Include a ruler, measuring tape, pasta claw, tongs, and plastic fork. Give her small containers such as a pill bottle and a small gift

bag to stuff and sort some of the yarn. Give her a ball of yarn to unravel! Include a sheet of coarse sandpaper so that your toddler can attach pieces of yarn to it. Include large plastic knitting needles or a plastic crochet hook. Cut a cardboard square and begin wrapping some yarn around it. Leave the rest of the yarn dangling to see if your toddler will continue wrapping the wool. Add items made from yarn: mittens, scarf, and sweater. After her own explorations, show her how to create lines and circles with the yarn.

SUPPLEMENTARY ACTIVITY:
Give your toddler a sheet of card stock paper or a paper plate. Add some double sided tape or glue over the surface. Give your child a bowl filled with various lengths of yarn to make a collage.

Lay a long piece of yarn on the floor and invite her to carefully walk along it. Make a large circle with yarn and walk around it.

SNACK:
Buy some string cheese and let him enjoy pulling off each strip and pretending it is yarn.

LETTER Z: ZOO

People go to the zoo and they like the lion because it's scary. And the bear because it's intense, but the monkey makes people laugh.

- Lorne Michaels

BOOKS TO READ:
Curious George Goes to the Zoo by Cynthia Platt
Good Night Gorilla by Peggy Rathmann
Never Ever Shout In A Zoo by Karma Wilson
My Trip To The Zoo by Mercer Mayer
My "x, y, z" Book by Jane Moncure

SENSORY BIN:
Pour into your container a combination of dried lentils and dried beans. Include one or two floral craft foams. Add a small dish of gem stones that can be a substitute for water and in another dish, add some green pompoms for food. Use some small boxes for

Sensory Play

the animals' homes. In a separate container, place plastic fencing, zoo animals, trucks, toy people, plastic trees, and artificial leaves.

SUPPLEMENTARY ACTIVITY:
Give your child some stamps or small trays of colored paints. Place on the table a selection of her zoo animals. He can create animal foot prints on a sheet of paper.

Print a Zoo Animals Matching Game from the following web-site:
http://www.nuttinbutpreschool.com/zoo-animal-printables-for-block-corner-or-matching-game/

Take your toddler to the zoo.

SNACK:
You will need a box of animal crackers. Spread some peanut butter on several pieces of celery. Get your toddler to insert an animal cracker on each piece of celery. Then give him

raisins and small pieces of fruit to place on the celery for the animal's food.

OTHER BOOKS

Busy Toddler, Happy Mom: Over 280 Activities to Engage Your Toddler in Small Motor and Gross Motor Activities, Crafts, Language Development and Sensory Play

COMING SOON

Traveling With Toddlers

Sign Up for the Busy Toddler, Happy Mom Newsletter at busytoddlerhappymom.com to receive more Toddler Activities and Updates on New Books.

ABOUT THE AUTHORS

Gayle Jervis has been writing curriculum ever since she taught English at a public school. She participated in starting a new course called Perspectives For Living and much of what she wrote was taken province wide to help other new teachers teach this course. When Gayle and her husband began their own family, she began writing curriculum for her own young children. When she decided to home school, her curriculum writing increased as she needed to find ways to teach two children who had two very different learning styles. During this time, she became involved in a local home school association and she became their librarian determined to build up their resources to help other home school parents. She also published a monthly newsletter for its members. Later, she became president of the association and during those two years, she hosted a large provincial home school conference. Now as her children have started their own families, she has begun once again to write appropriate curriculum especially for her two toddler grandchildren. It is her heart's desire to help moms of young toddlers to harness the energy of their little people and to develop those necessary skills to prepare them for preschool.

Kristen Jervis Cacka graduated from university in business with the intention of starting her own business. However, she changed her plans when she met her husband and instead she has been enjoying staying at home with her lovely daughter. Therefore, as Kristen began looking for appropriate materials for her young toddler, she became frustrated by the lack of fun curriculum that could be used in a home setting. That was when she and her mom, Gayle, decided to collaborate their talents and create a series of books not only meeting her goals for her own daughter but helping other moms looking for similar activities.

WORKS CITED

"'And in the end it is not the years in your life that count, it's the life in your years.'."*Goodreads*. 07 Aug. 2013 <http://www.goodreads.com/quotes/2712-and-in-the-end-it-is-not-the-years-in>.

"Art Quotes by Clyde Aspevig - Art Quotes - The Painter's Keys Resource of Art Quotations." Art Quotes by Clyde Aspevig - Art Quotes - The Painter's Keys Resource of Art Quotations. 07 Aug. 2013 <http://quote.robertgenn.com/auth_search.php?authid=6493>.

"'Autumn is a second spring when every leaf is a flower.'."*Goodreads*. 07 Aug. 2013 <http://www.goodreads.com/quotes/32925-autumn-is-a-second-spring-when-every-leaf-is-a>.

"Crayon Quotes, Sayings about Colors, Coloring, Crayons, etc." Crayon Quotes, Sayings about Colors, Coloring, Crayons, etc. 07 Aug. 2013 <http://www.quotegarden.com/crayons.html>.

"'Do not abandon yourselves to despair. We are the Easter people and hallelujah is our song.'." Goodreads. 07 Aug. 2013 <http://www.goodreads.com/quotes/245044-do-not-abandon-yourselves-to-despair-we-are-the-easter>.

"'Each day I live in a glass room unless I break it with the thrusting of my senses and pass through the splintered walls to the great landscape.'." *Goodreads*. 07 Aug. 2013 <http://www.goodreads.com/quotes/261541-each-day-i-live-in-a-glass-room-unless-i>.

"Edward Sandford Martin Quotes & Sayings." Search Quotes. 07 Aug. 2013
<http://www.searchquotes.com/quotation/Thanksgiving_Day_comes,_by_statute,_once_a_year;_to_the_honest_man_it_comes_as_frequently_as_the_hea/294383/>.

"Fire Quotes, Sayings about Fires, Fire Safety." *Quote Garden*. 08 Aug. 2013
<http://www.quotegarden.com/fire.html>.

"Frank Sinatra Quotes & Sayings." *Search Quotes*. 07 Aug. 2013
<http://www.searchquotes.com/quotation/Orange_is_the_happiest_color./221034/>.

""For ourselves, who are ordinary men and women, let us return thanks to Nature for her bounty by using every one of the senses she has given us."." *Goodreads*. 07 Aug. 2013
<http://www.goodreads.com/quotes/300001-for-ourselves-who-are-ordinary-men-and-women-let-us>.

"Green Eggs and Ham Quotes." Dr. Seuss. 08 Aug. 2013
<http://www.goodreads.com/work/quotes/86934-green-eggs-and-ham>.

"Green Fairy Quilts." *Green Fairy Quilts*. 08 Aug. 2013
<http://greenfairyquilts.com/pages/-QuiltingQuotes.php>.

"Green is the prime color of... by Pedro Calderon de la Barca, a Spanish Dramatist | GoodQuotes.com." Green is the prime color of... by Pedro Calderon de la Barca, a Spanish Dramatist | GoodQuotes.com. 07 Aug. 2013
<http://www.goodquotes.com/quote/pedro-calderon-de-la-barca/green-is-the-prime-color-of-the-world>.

"Homer Simpson Quotes & Sayings." *Search Quotes*. 07 Aug. 2013 <http://www.searchquotes.com/quotation/This_donut_has_purple_in_the_middle%2C_purple_is_a_fruit./265265/>.

"'I am a Canadian, free to speak without fear, free to worship in my own way, free to stand for what I think right, free to oppose what I believe wrong, or free to choose those who shall govern my country. This heritage of freedom I pledge to uphold for myself and all mankind.'." Goodreads. 07 Aug. 2013 <http://www.goodreads.com/quotes/521518-i-am-a-canadian-free-to-speak-without-fear-free>.

"I claim there ain't Another Saint As great as Valentine." Very Best Quotes com. 07 Aug. 2013 <http://www.verybestquotes.com/i-claim-there-aint-another-saint-as-great-as-valentine/>.

"If Ants Are Such Busy Workers How Come They Find Time To Go To All The Picnics Quotes." Search Quotes. 08 Aug. 2013 <http://www.searchquotes.com/quotation/If_ants_are_such_busy_workers,_how_come_they_find_time_to_go_to_all_the_picnics?/127080/>.

"'If all the insects were to disappear from the earth, within 50 years all life on earth would end. If all human beings disappeared from the earth, within 50 years all forms of life would flourish.'."*Goodreads*. 08 Aug. 2013 <http://www.goodreads.com/quotes/494755-if-all-the-insects-were-to-disappear-from-the-earth>.

"'If you have a garden and a library, you have everything you need.'." The Quote Factory. 08 Aug. 2013

<http://www.thequotefactory.com/quote-by/marcus-tullius-cicero/if-you-have-a-garden-and-a-library/41030>.

"Island Ireland: Irish Blessings & Prayers." Island Ireland: Irish Blessings & Prayers. 07 Aug. 2013 <http://www.islandireland.com/Pages/folk/sets/bless.html>.

"It's no use carrying an umbrella if your shoes are leaking." *The Quotations Page*. 08 Aug. 2013 <http://www.quotationspage.com/quote/37607.html>.

"It is a wise father that knows his own child... on Quotations Book." Quote - It is a wise father that knows his own child... on Quotations Book. 07 Aug. 2013 <http://quotationsbook.com/quote/14595/>.

""I've always felt there is something sacred in a piece of paper that travels the earth from hand to hand, head to head, heart to heart."." *Goodreads*. 08 Aug. 2013 <http://www.goodreads.com/quotes/619156-i-ve-always-felt-there-is-something-sacred-in-a-piece>.

"John Geddes Quotes." John Geddes Quotes (Author of Highway to Hell). 07 Aug. 2013 <https://www.goodreads.com/author/quotes/199199.John_Geddes>.

"John McCrae Quotes & Sayings." Search Quotes. 07 Aug. 2013 <http://www.searchquotes.com/quotation/In_Flanders_fields_the_poppies_blow_Between_the_crosses,_row_on_row_That_mark_our_place;_and_in_the_/242289/>.

"Kids don't like being put into boxes, and your kid can act in different ways in different situations." *BrainyQuote*.

Xplore. 08 Aug. 2013
<http://www.brainyquote.com/quotes/quotes/r/rosalind wi497558.html>.

"''Kites rise highest against the wind, not with it.''." *Goodreads*. 08 Aug. 2013
<http://www.goodreads.com/quotes/11419-kites-rise-highest-against-the-wind-not-with-it>.

"Knitting Rules! Quotes." By Stephanie Pearl-McPhee. 08 Aug. 2013
<http://www.goodreads.com/work/quotes/120225-knitting-rules-the-yarn-harlot-s-bag-of-knitting-tricks>.

"Ladybug Quotes, Sayings about Ladybugs." *Quote Garden*. 08 Aug. 2013
<http://www.quotegarden.com/ladybugs.html>.

"Lee Greenwood Quotes & Sayings." Search Quotes. 07 Aug. 2013
<http://www.searchquotes.com/quotation/And_I'm_proud_to_be_an_American,_where_at_least_I_know_I'm_free,_and_I_won't_forget_the_men_who_died/277022/>.

"Luke 2:16-17." *Holy Bible: New International Version*. Grand Rapids, MI: Zondervan, 2005.

"Motherhood: All love begins... by Robert Browning, an English Poet | GoodQuotes.com." Motherhood: All love begins... by Robert Browning, an English Poet | GoodQuotes.com. 07 Aug. 2013
<http://www.goodquotes.com/quote/robert-browning/motherhood-all-love-begins-and-ends-th>.

"''One must ask children and birds how cherries and strawberries taste.''." *Goodreads*. 08 Aug. 2013

<http://www.goodreads.com/quotes/81575-one-must-ask-children-and-birds-how-cherries-and-strawberries>.

"People go to the zoo and they like the lion because it's scary. And the bear because it's intense, but the monkey makes people laugh." *BrainyQuote*. 08 Aug. 2013 <http://www.brainyquote.com/quotes/authors/l/lorne_michaels.html>.

"Peter Benchley Quotes & Sayings." *Search Quotes*. 08 Aug. 2013
<http://www.searchquotes.com/quotation/I_believe_implicitly_that_every_young_man_in_the_world_is_fascinated_with_either_sharks_or_dinosaurs/58958/>.

"'Pink isn't just a color it's an Attitude too!'." *Goodreads*. 07 Aug. 2013
<http://www.goodreads.com/quotes/287717-pink-isn-t-just-a-color-it-s-an-attitude-too>.

"Professional Quotes." Quotes by Diana Vreeland at Quotes4Life.net. 07 Aug. 2013
<http://www.quotes4life.net/authors/d/Diana-Vreeland>.

"Pulling Good Times Out of a Hat." *The New York Times*. 8 Aug. 2013
<http://www.nytimes.com/2009/02/26/fashion/26ROW.html>.

"Quote - Life on a farm is a school of patience; you can't hurry the crops or make an ox in two days... on Quotations Book." Quotations Book. 08 Aug. 2013
<http://quotationsbook.com/quote/14413/>.

"Raoul Dufy, 1877 - 1953." Raoul Dufy quotes from QOTD.org (page 1 of 1). 07 Aug. 2013 <http://www.qotd.org/search/search.html?aid=5684>.

"Related quotes." Patrick Thompson Famous Quote about Identify, Patterns, Researchers, Shell, Turtles. 08 Aug. 2013 <http://www.quotesdaddy.com/quote/811120/Patrick Thompson/researchers-identify-turtles-by-the-different-patterns>.

"Robert H Schuller Quotes & Sayings." *Search Quotes*. 08 Aug. 2013 <http://www.searchquotes.com/quotation/Anyone_can_count_the_seeds_in_an_apple,_but_only_God_can_count_the_number_of_apples_in_a_seed./2720/>.

"Sarah Kay Quotes." Sarah Kay Quotes (Author of B). 08 Aug. 2013 <http://www.goodreads.com/author/quotes/11377.Sarah_Kay>.

""Senses empower limitations, senses expand vision within borders, senses promote understanding through pleasure."."*Goodreads*. 08 Aug. 2013 <http://www.goodreads.com/quotes/590275-senses-empower-limitations-senses-expand-vision-within-borders-senses-promote>.

""Spring is nature's way of saying, Let's party!"." *Goodreads*. 07 Aug. 2013 <http://www.goodreads.com/quotes/32958-spring-is-nature-s-way-of-saying-let-s-party>.

"Stefan Kanfer Quotes & Sayings." *Search Quotes*. 07 Aug. 2013

<http://www.searchquotes.com/quotation/There's_something_strange_and_powerful_about_black-and-white_imagery./87407/>.

"Steve Almond Quotes." - Quotables. 07 Aug. 2013 <http://quotabl.es/quotes/by/steve-almond>.

""Summer afternoon-summer afternoon; to me those have always been the two most beautiful words in the English language."." *Goodreads*. 07 Aug. 2013 <http://www.goodreads.com/quotes/63388-summer-afternoon-summer-afternoon-to-me-those-have-always-been-the>.

"Tahir Shah Quotes." Tahir Shah Quotes (Author of The Caliph's House). 08 Aug. 2013 <http://www.goodreads.com/author/quotes/7102.Tahir_Shah>.

"The best doctor in the world is a veterinarian. He can't ask his patients what is the matter - - he's got to just know." *Quotes of Will Rogers*. 08 Aug. 2013 <http://www.willrogers.com/says/will_says.html>.

""The color brown, I realized, is anything but nondescript. It comes in as many hues as there are colors of earth, with is commonly presumed infinite."." *Goodreads*. 07 Aug. 2013 <http://www.goodreads.com/quotes/571212-the-color-brown-i-realized-is-anything-but-nondescript-it>.

"The message is not so much that the worms will inherit the Earth, but that all things play a role in nature, even the lowly worm." *Cartoonist Quotes*. 08 Aug. 2013 <http://www.quotesfriend.com/cartoonist-quotes.html>.

""Touch comes before sight, before speech. It is the first language and the last, and it always tells the truth."." *Goodreads*. 07 Aug. 2013 <http://www.goodreads.com/quotes/112626-touch-comes-before-sight-before-speech-it-is-the-first>.

"W T Purkiser Quotes & Sayings." Search Quotes. 07 Aug. 2013 <http://www.searchquotes.com/quotation/Not_what_we_say_about_our_blessings,_but_how_we_use_them,_is_the_true_measure_of_our_thanksgiving./25815/>.

""What are men to rocks and mountains?"." *Goodreads*. 08 Aug. 2013 <http://www.goodreads.com/quotes/6528-what-are-men-to-rocks-and-mountains>.

"William Osler Quotes & Sayings." Search Quotes. 08 Aug. 2013 <http://www.searchquotes.com/quotation/The_trained_nurse_has_become_one_of_the_great_blessings_of_humanity,_taking_a_place_beside_the_physi/474562/>.

"Winter Quotes, Wintertime Sayings." Winter Quotes, Wintertime Sayings. 07 Aug. 2013 <http://www.quotegarden.com/winter.html>.

"Without black, no color has any depth. But if you mix..." *Quote Wise*. 07 Aug. 2013 <http://www.quote-wise.com/quotes/amy-grant/without-black-no-color-has-any-depth-but-if-y>.

"Wordsworth, William. 1888. Complete Poetical Works." Wordsworth, William. 1888. Complete Poetical Works. 07 Aug. 2013 <http://www.bartleby.com/145/ww194.html>.

"Yellow Color Quotes." *The Quotes Tree*. 07 Aug. 2013 <http://www.quotestree.com/yellow-color-quotes.html>.

"Yo Ho (A Pirate's Life for Me)." *Wikipedia*. 08 May 2013. Wikimedia Foundation. 08 Aug. 2013 <http://en.wikipedia.org/wiki/Yo_Ho_%28A_Pirate%27s_Life_for_Me%29>.

"You can teach a student a lesson for a day; but if you can teach him to learn by creating curiosity, he will continue the learning process as long as he lives. by Clay P. Bedford." Quote World. 07 Aug. 2013 <http://www.quoteworld.org/quotes/1112>.

INDEX

A

ANTS · 172
APPLES · 110

B

BACK TO SCHOOL · 144
BIRDS · 175
BIRTHDAYS · 142
BLACK · 64
BLACK AND WHITE · 69
BLUE · 39
BOAT RIDES · 104
BOX · 238
BROWN · 61

C

CAMPING · 178
CANADA DAY · 137
CATERPILLARS AND BUTTERFLIES · 94
CHICKS AND EGGS · 91
CHINESE NEW YEAR · 121
COLORFUL LEAVES · 107

D

DECORATING FOR CHRISTMAS · 157
DINOSAURS · 181

E

EASTER · 130
EGGS · 184

F

FARM · 186
FATHER'S DAY · 135

G

GARDEN · 188
GONE FISHING · 100
GREEN · 42

H

HALLOWEEN · 149
HATS · 191

I

ICE SKATING · 86
INDEPENDENCE DAY · 140
INSECTS · 194

J

JUNGLE · 197

K

KALEIDOSCOPE OF COLORS · 71
KITES · 200

L

LADYBUGS · 203

M

MAIL · 206
MIXED COLORS · 47
MOTHER'S DAY · 133

N

NATIVITY · 160
NURSES · 209

O

OCEANS · 212
ORANGE · 57

P

PINK · 54
PIRATES · 215
PUMPKINS · 112
PURPLE · 50

Q

QUILTS · 218

R

RAINBOW COLORS · 59
Recipe for Colored Rice or Colored Pasta · 16
RED · 36
REMEMBRANCE DAY/VETERAN'S DAY · 154
ROCKS · 221

S

SEASHELLS BY THE SEASHORE · 102
SEEDS · 224
SNOW · 83
SPRING RAIN · 97
ST. PATRICK'S DAY · 127

T

THANKSGIVING · 146
THANKSGIVING (USA) · 151
TURTLES · 227

U

UMBRELLAS · 230

V

VALENTINE'S DAY · 124

VETERINARIANS · 233

___

W

WHITE · 66
WINTER ANIMALS · 88
WORMS · 236

___

Y

YARN · 241
YELLOW · 44

___

Z

ZOO · 244

Made in the USA
San Bernardino, CA
30 June 2015